listen

[Trusting Your Inner Voice in Times of Crisis]

With caring, candor and humor, Lynn reminds us that we each have an inner compass that always points us in the right direction. Read *LISTEN* and hear its wisdom.

—Marci Shimoff, *New York Times* bestselling author, *Happy for No Reason* and *Chicken Soup for the Woman's Soul*

An extraordinarily clear, no-nonsense, down-to-earth, utterly practical, doable, and believable guide to accessing the extraordinary wisdom you already own. The many real-life examples and stimulating exercises offer a golden map to live the life your heart truly desires. I heartily recommend *LISTEN* to anyone wishing for more inner peace, joy, and success.

—Alan Cohen, author, *I Had It All the Time*

LISTEN is a valuable resource for anyone who is experiencing a crisis, a life transition, or is simply feeling stuck.

—Judith Orloff MD, author, *Emotional Freedom*

Listen up! You can trust your still, quiet inner voice for wise guidance when things fall apart, and renowned intuitive Lynn Robinson shows us how in *LISTEN*. In this spiritually intelligent new book, we have instructions for accessing divine wisdom in these volatile and challenging times. I recommend it heartily.

—Lama Surya Das, Buddhist spiritual leader, author, *Awakening the Buddha Within*

I credit Lynn Robinson with giving me permission to trust my intuition and techniques for hearing the inner voice. In *LISTEN,* she demystifies this sixth sense so we can use it to make a positive difference in real life.

—Victoria Moran, author, *Living a Charmed Life*

Wisdom is not a pumping in of information from the outside. It is a realization that comes from within, reminding us of what we have known all along. *LISTEN* will guide you inward, tapping you in to your greatest knowing.

—Elisabeth Fayt, author, *Paving It Forward,* and Founder of RnR Wellness Spa Chain

Your own intuition is the key to your health and happiness and *LISTEN* will help you to put this into practice. Lynn Robinson has a rare gift for melding the practical and the spiritual. You can feel her wisdom and experience on every page. Once you have read it, keep this book handy. You'll use it again and again.

—Jonathan Ellerby PhD, author, *Return to the Sacred: Ancient Pathways to Spiritual Awakening*

LISTEN shows you how to recognize, trust and take action on your intuitive wisdom. Lynn shares stories, techniques and encouragement that will help you live a joyous and abundant life.

—Matthew B. James, MA, PhD, President, American Pacific University

As I read Lynn's new book, *LISTEN,* I felt as if I were tweeting with a best friend. Line-by-line, little snippets of compassionate wisdom, wonderful stories and useful techniques were revealed. The fact that Lynn figured out how to package-up "intuition" in such a highly useful format, designed to help us all through good times and bad, is alone something worth tweeting about!

—Dan Hollings, Internet, Social Media Twitter Strategist; Internet Strategist for the hit movie *The Secret*

listen

[Trusting Your Inner Voice in Times of Crisis]

LYNN A. ROBINSON

gpp®
life

Guilford, Connecticut

To Gary
Thank you for being my wonderful companion
and soul mate on the path of life.

To Cliff
You have a strong and vital inner compass.
Keep trusting it! It's guiding you unerringly. I'm very proud of you.

To buy books in quantity for corporate use
or incentives, call **(800) 962–0973**
or e-mail **premiums@GlobePequot.com.**

GPP Life is an imprint of Globe Pequot Press.

Designed by Sheryl P. Kober

Library of Congress Cataloging-in-Publication Data is available on file.

ISBN 978-0-7627-5251-5

Printed in the United States of America

10 9 8 7 6 5 4 3 2 1

Contents

The whisper holds the answer, it's up to me to ask
I wonder why so often, the thing that I do last is . . .
Listen for the whisper deep down inside
Listen for the whisper, a strong but gentle guide
With a thousand different voices ringing in my ear
I listen for the whisper that only the heart can hear.

From the song, "Listen for the Whisper"
by Jana Stanfield, Tony Harrell
www.JanaStanfield.com

Introduction

We live in a time of turmoil and upheaval. The stability we've counted on—steady jobs, long-lived marriages, excellent health, financial security—is a thing of the past for many of us. So where are the directions to find sanity and safety amidst all this loss? You'll find them within you. They've been there all along. We just seem to have forgotten where to look.

This book is about helping you tap into and listen to your source of wisdom. You have inside information that gives you accurate guidance to make the best choices for a happy career, to improve your marriage, to help your kids, to live a healthy life full of hope, passion, and purpose. Most important, it can help you get your life back on track when you're been thrown off course.

This wisdom doesn't come from your logical mind. It comes from a spiritual source that you may experience as an inner prompting, an inspiration, a gut feeling, a quickening, a knowing deep in your heart. It doesn't speak to you through a megaphone or in a loud voice. It fact, most often it communicates through the proverbial "still, quiet, inner voice."

You don't go through this life alone. You are constantly receiving inner guidance. You are attuned to the frequency of this message by being still and listening within. The guidance may not be received at the exact moment you're tuning in, but it's there, giving you solace, direction, and loving counsel throughout every moment of the day and night.

"Be still and know that I am God," is a frequently quoted phrase from the Bible. What does it mean? It's inviting you to slow down, take a few deep breaths, and attune to the Source in whatever way feels right to you. It's affirming that there is a Wisdom in the universe that has created all sorts of wonderful and miraculous things. It's acknowledging that this Source has your best interests at heart and can give you guidance and solace when you most need it.

Why do we go through these difficult times? The answer, as many religions tell us, is "only God knows." However, I have long observed that we are on the path to our greatest potential when we're the most uncomfortable. There's something about those times of crisis that catapult us out of our self-imposed comfort zones and compel us to connect with our larger purpose, with each other, and with the spiritual source of all things.

When you're experiencing a challenging time, it's common to wonder, "Will life ever return to normal?" When you allow yourself to be gently led by your intuition, you're putting your faith and trust in Divine hands. This Source can see the big picture for your life and knows the best path to get you where you need to go—back to a sense of peace—no matter what is happening in your life.

Go within to a quiet place in your heart and simply ask for guidance. Wait with patience and confidence. The answers will come. You're always being guided to the next right job, a shift in attitude, a path to create a more loving relationship, or a way to heal your body. The answer may arrive as a huge surprise, leaving you excited and exhilarated. It may also come as a simple nudge or prompting, gently guiding you to something new. There is no right or wrong way to receive this insight.

We need to listen to this wisdom now more than ever. Open your heart and mind to the brilliance within you. Let it guide your life. You are being gently and surely led. There is always a way home.

The pages that follow will assist you on your journey. So take this book, settle in to a place of comfort and peace, and then become quiet. Listen . . .

CHAPTER 1

When Your World Turns Upside Down

The rays of happiness, like those of light,
are colorless when unbroken.
—HENRY WADSWORTH LONGFELLOW

- No one escapes it.
- It will happen to you at least once in your life.
- It's scary, it's frightening, and it'll make you wonder whether you'll ever be the same.
- It makes you feel like you're going crazy.
- It makes you wish for your old life, however difficult it may have been.
- You will think no one else has ever gone through it and survived.
- You wake up at 3:00 a.m. and it sets in.
- You may not talk about it to anyone. Who would understand?
- You think there is something wrong with you. Why can't you just turn it around?

What is it? Quite simply, your world has turned upside down. There may have been any number of things that pushed you into this nightmare . . .

There's a merger at the company you've worked at for more than a decade. You've been an exemplary team member. It's been intimated that the merger may actually result in a long-overdue promotion. You're totally unprepared when your boss takes you aside one Friday afternoon and tells you your job has been eliminated. You've got two kids to support and you've been living paycheck-to-paycheck.

Or,

You're having a routine physical exam and your doctor notices a small lump on your right breast. Probably nothing to worry about; the recent mammogram didn't show anything. But she schedules you for a biopsy to make sure. A week later you receive the call asking you to come see her to discuss the results. You have breast cancer.

Or,

You and your husband have had your share of difficulties, but you've always worked them out. You've got two great kids whom you adore; you're proud of their achievements, and you look forward to seeing them grow up. One Sunday evening you're checking your e-mail before retiring for the night and discover your husband has left a file open on the desktop. You're shocked to read his note. It's to an old girlfriend with graphic details of a recent visit. When you confront him, he breaks down in tears and tells you he wants a divorce.

The life-changing event may be a total surprise. Or, it may be one that you've chosen. You're the one announcing you want out of the marriage, to change your career, to go back to school, or to move to a different part of the country. Whatever the circumstances, your life has turned upside down.

You may also find yourself at a crossroads because of general economic uncertainty, war, or environmental disasters. These and many more crises are what this book is about. How do you make wise decisions when your life is turned upside down? How do you find peace, calm, and sanity again? Whom do you trust when the "experts" give you conflicting advice? How do you discern the choices that will lead to success and not more failure?

It's frightening, scary, and anxiety producing to go through any of these life changes. You probably know someone who has gone through a divorce, changed careers, or had a serious illness. How did they make it through? How did they turn their lives right-side up again?

It often feels like being lost in the woods. There are no obvious markers that say, "this way to safety." If you look up the word transition in the dictionary, you'll see definitions like "passing from one to another," a "passage," "major change," "shift," and "development." All these words indicate transformation. It's what life requires of us.

When you're going through one of these life-changing events, you may worry that you're falling apart and might be in this limbo forever. You may feel trapped with nowhere to go—and yet it's that uncomfortable shift from one place in your life to the next where the most transformation can occur.

Everyone experiences transition, often many times, during the course of a lifetime. It feels unpleasant because it requires that you let go of the known, the familiar, what you've come to think of as safe. You know where you've been but you don't know where you're headed. Many people deal with this discomfort by trying to go back to the familiar. But it's like trying to stuff the toothpaste back into the tube. You want the old job back, or you attempt to reestablish a relationship that is no longer viable.

For the past twenty-plus years, I've worked as an intuitive adviser. People call me when they're in the midst of change or transition. I use my intuition and help them use theirs to gain clarity; to figure out their next steps or determine what might be standing in their way. Many of the calls I receive for consultations are from people who are contemplating a career change; beginning or ending a relationship; or are coping with a tangible or intangible loss of some kind in their lives.

I frequently hear people telling me that they feel adrift. They wish for an instruction book to help them make sense of their crisis—a book that would tell them about their life purpose and lessons, inform them about the best career choices, make clear who to marry (and who not to!), as well as provide detailed information about how to stay happy and healthy throughout the years.

Your Instruction Book for Life

However, I've come to believe that we do, in fact, have those instructions. We've always had them. They're written in our souls. We're hardwired to receive this information. It's called intuition—a ready source of direction, a compass of the soul—available to all of us. This Divine wisdom is an invisible intelligence that animates our world and provides insight and direction to guide our lives. Someone once said, "Prayer is when we speak to God. Intuition is one of the ways our prayers are answered."

Listen is about how we hear this wise guidance. Some of what you'll read on these pages will be my own experiences from the "school of hard knocks." You'll also hear from many others as they share their life stories, along with insight about how they followed their inner compass to get going in the right direction again. In preparation for writing this book,

I created a "Life Transition Survey." I heard from more than a thousand people who volunteered information about their own life changes and how they coped with the anxiety, fear, and stress they experienced. I found it so life affirming to read and hear about the tools, techniques, and inner resources that people used to turn their lives in a positive direction again. I hope you'll feel inspired, too! I've changed the names and details in some of these stories to protect the privacy of the individuals involved.

At the end of each chapter, you'll find an Intuition Journal exercise. You may want to buy a special notebook especially assigned for the purpose. The exercises are usually questions that are intended to act as writing prompts to elicit information from your own fabulous intuitive guidance system. The questions (and your answers) will help you understand, in a practical way, what you've just read. They take just a few minutes of your time, and I urge you to give them a try. Who knows? You may discover something about yourself or your world that will make a surprisingly positive difference in your life. My wish is that *Listen* will help you tap into your innate wisdom and fill you with hope, inspiration, and direction to live the fulfilling life you were meant to live.

A Word about the Word *God*

Throughout the book I use the word *God* to refer to what some call a Universal Consciousness. I use other words, too, but I recognize that *God* may be problematic for many. If you are among those who have trouble with this word, then I hope you'll substitute a term such as Universe, Spirit, Divine Wisdom, Higher Power, or whatever else works for you.

When you are going through a crisis, God is helping you move the old, resistant places in yourself to allow something new, fresh, and invigorating to take its place. There's an old saying: "When everything is breaking up, something new is breaking through." I've found that, as difficult as it is, the most helpful attitude to take during these times is to embrace the transition. (If it were only as easy as it sounds!) The one true thing about transitions is that they have an end. You will land on solid ground once again. It will just be in a different place than you've ever been before. By listening to your wisdom within, you are led to the right path.

Author Margaret Drabble wrote, "When nothing is sure, everything is possible." The fact that you're uncomfortable doesn't mean you're doing something wrong. It just means that change is happening and you—like most people—feel anxious when it occurs. The life challenge you're experiencing can be a very creative time. Your life is up in the air, but anything and everything is possible.

> ## When nothing is sure, everything is possible.

What Is Intuition?

The dictionary defines it as "quick and ready insight." It comes from the Latin root *intueri,* which means "to look within." I think of intuition as a compass of the soul that guides, informs, and directs us toward success. It's a skill we all have. We use it to make successful decisions and choices as well as to stay clear of danger. We're born with intuition. Perhaps some of us have the ability to tap into it more easily than others. But as with any skill, the more we practice using it, the better we get at it.

What is this gift of intuition? How do others define it? Here are some ways it's commonly described:

- A tool for quick and ready insight
- A natural mental faculty
- A gut feeling
- A sixth sense
- An inner knowing
- A hunch
- Wisdom from a Higher Power
- A still, quiet inner voice

There Are Many Ways to Receive Intuitive Information

As the title of this book suggests, we often hear these intuitive messages and need to listen for the wisdom. It's referred to as the "still, quiet, inner voice." That's how Ellen received the information that ultimately led to her diagnosis of breast cancer. She had just gotten the all-clear from her doctor after getting her yearly mammogram and was told to check back next year.

I didn't have any signs or symptoms of cancer. I was just having my regular checkup. So I wasn't particularly surprised when my doctor said I was fine. However, when I got in my car to drive home, I heard what I can only describe as an inner voice that said, "Get this checked again."

I'm a very practical, grounded, and scientifically oriented person. I'm not typically given to hearing voices, especially ones that contradict my trusted doctor's findings. Over the next few days, I simply found that I couldn't get that message out of my head. It was bugging me so much that I decided to pay out-of-pocket for a second mammogram.

I was shocked when I heard the results. The second radiologist had found a very small but suspicious mass in my left breast. A biopsy later confirmed the results. I had stage 1 breast cancer. Fortunately, my cancer was caught early, and with surgery, radiation, and a short course of chemotherapy I have an excellent chance of long-term survival. I shudder to think about what might have happened if I hadn't listened to my intuition.

Jan also receives information through an intuitive knowing. She describes it as a "felt sense" that was invaluable in guiding her through a difficult divorce.

I was devastated when my husband asked for a divorce. I'd been a stay-at-home mom with two boys ages seven and nine. I was completely shocked when my husband told me he had met someone else and wanted out of the marriage.

I sobbed myself to sleep every night for weeks after that initial conversation. I seemed to have no clue how to find a job, get myself together, take care of the kids, deal with our changed lives, and start over. Reading personal growth books was my salvation during that time. I read [your book] Divine Intuition *and decided to try meditation and listening to my intuition.*

I can't tell you that things changed overnight, but I began to feel as if my inner wisdom was guiding me. I committed to taking small steps every day to help me find a job and to stay sane for myself and the boys. It wasn't easy. I'm a very spiritual person, and I was angry at God for allowing this to happen to me, to us. However, I chose to believe that I had an inner wisdom directing me and put my trust in the process and knew that I'd be guided to a better situation.

It's now a year since that initial conversation with my husband. I have a new job working in customer service at a local bank, we're renting a nice apartment, and I have hopes that after the divorce is final, I'll be able to buy a home. Intuition also guided me in helping me heal the discord with my husband. So even though we're still proceeding with a divorce, he's very involved with the kids and we have an amicable relationship.

A year ago I couldn't have imagined saying this, but I'm much happier now. I feel like a good life is ahead of me, options are open, and I'm a better person and mom to my kids. I also know I can count on my inner guidance to get me through tough times.

As Jan implies, times of transition are a study in contradiction. At the point you want to rail at God for causing this change in your life, you also need to trust the wisdom of this same Force to bring about the transformation you need. Intuition is extremely helpful in transition, as it will point the way to the path that will take you to your new life. The poet Rainer Maria Rilke noted, "The future enters into us, in order to transform us, long before it happens." Life requires transformation. Let's begin . . .

> **The future enters into us, in order to transform us, long before it happens.**

Intuition is the subliminal sense that spirit endowed us with to maneuver safely through the maze of real life.
—SARAH BAN BREATHNACH

YOUR INTUITION JOURNAL

Each of us has our own unique way of receiving intuitive information. Write in your journal about a time when your intuition guided a decision. How did you receive the information? Did you receive an image, a dream, a feeling, or did you simply "just know" the answer?

CHAPTER 2

The Many Ways to Listen

Learn to get in touch with the silence within yourself,
and know that everything in this life has a purpose.
There are no mistakes. No coincidences. All events are
blessings given to us to learn from.
—ELISABETH KÜBLER-ROSS

Let's face it: Most of us don't have the time, inclination, or aptitude for a weeklong meditation retreat when we need to tune in to our inner wisdom. So what do you do when you're in the midst of a crisis and have only small moments of time to seek the silence within for answers and direction? In this chapter I'll provide you with resources, exercises, and ideas to help you hear and trust your intuition. Sometimes it's as simple as pushing yourself away from your desk and taking a few deep, calming breaths.

The journey to spiritual wisdom is an inner one. To hear and trust Spirit more clearly, you have to take the time to listen. One of the best-known phrases from the Bible is Psalms 46:10: "Be still and know that I am God." If you're experiencing a time of crisis, you're probably finding yourself rushing around, filled with anxiety and stress. What's the antidote to this? "Be still."

Many spiritual traditions speak of letting go and surrendering to a Higher Power that can guide us to safety and peace. It starts simply with being still and turning inward toward God in whatever way feels right to you.

The Importance of Stillness

The line "Be still and know that I am God" suggests that you begin with a quiet, attentive mind. When you are able to center yourself even within a busy, stress-filled day, your connection to God is assured. You are building

and opening the channel to receive Divine wisdom and direction. The stillness doesn't need to come in the form of a long meditation unless that
practice is attractive to you. It can come just as effectively in small slivers
of time.

You form a deeper relationship with God by creating a silent space
within yourself. This means that you'll need to find a way to retreat from
all the noise of both your external life and the cacophony of your inner
thoughts. The French philosopher Pascal once said, "All man's troubles
stem from his inability to sit quietly in a room alone."

There are so many ways to listen. There's no one way that's the "right"
way. Find ways to make this connection with God interesting, creative,
and light. Any discipline that guides you to be present in the here and now
and connects you to Spirit is a good method. Some people find stillness by
sitting in meditation or prayer. Others may experience it while walking in
the woods or even by taking a few centering breaths while sitting at their
desk in the office.

Pockets of Quietude

In our culture we believe that doing, taking action, and making the effort
are the most important ways to get out of a crisis. What if the opposite is
true? What if you give yourself permission to simply be, and rest in order
to find peace and solutions to your current confusion? Learning to listen
requires two things: a practice that facilitates quieting your mind, such as
meditation, prayer, or communing with nature; and an understanding or
discovery of how you receive answers.

When you're in pain and suffering through a crisis, you want to fix it.
You'll do anything to get out of the misery of the experience. I've often
joked that I should invent a Rip van Winkle pill. You take it and wake up
when your crisis is over and all your lessons are learned. But what if this
crisis is really asking you to sit with the pain and listen to its message?
What's really going on? What is the experience trying to teach you? If you
can get to the heart of it, you'll prevent it from coming back in another
form. So before you take action, be still and listen within.

I read an article recently about best-selling author and management
consultant Jim Collins. He recommended creating what he called "pockets

of quietude" in your schedule. These can be small periods of time marked off on your schedule for self-reflection. It's an appointment with yourself to find an inner calm, tap into your center, and find creative solutions to difficult problems.

Pockets of quietude can also take the form of a day off, or several days off, when you need creative inspiration and self-reflection. Collins blocked these "white spaces" on his calendar. "I set them six months in advance, and everyone around me can see them. It's not that I'm not working, but absolutely nothing can be scheduled on a white space day." He also suggested that creating a "not-to-do list" is more important than a to-do list. Things on this list might include not attending a certain meeting or taking on a huge new project. His comment may sound overly simplistic. Yet how much of your day is spent in time-wasting activities that are inherently draining?

Taking those pockets of time can simply be a moment of brief prayer and contemplation. You might ask yourself questions such as "What's the most loving response to this situation?" or "How could I view this issue from a more spiritual perspective?" Pay attention to any response that makes you feel more peaceful or clear.

Find Sources of Inspiration

One of the ways that I make time for spiritual centering is to subscribe to an inspirational daily word. I like the print editions, but there are many online versions to choose from. If you type "inspirational newsletter" or "spiritual inspiration" into a search engine, you'll come up with a number of them. My favorites are *Science of Mind* and *Guideposts,* which I receive as monthly print magazines.

A recent affirmation from *Science of Mind* reads: "All the power and presence in the Universe is right where I am. I am always in a state of perfect equilibrium because I am receptive to the divine truth around me and in me." How perfect is that? I spend a few moments as I begin my day reading the text and affirmation and simply sitting with the wisdom. I find it very centering and calming.

How Others Create Quiet Time

How do you find time for the stillness within in the midst of a busy life? Can you tune in to God while you're driving to work, making dinner, or reading to the kids? I asked clients, friends, and newsletter subscribers these questions and received some wonderful answers. I've shared some of my favorites below.

Practice patience while driving.

"I spend a great deal of time on the road in my job as a salesman. I used to experience a lot of road rage. I was always angry! Now I try to see other drivers as people who may also be having a tough time. I see them as teachers of patience. I send them love. I wave them into my lane and let them go ahead of me. It may sound silly, but this shift in attitude has created an enormous oasis of peace in my car. And guess what—my sales have increased exponentially!"

Build quiet time into your day.

"I work in a busy office and make it a priority to eat lunch in a nearby park or, when the weather's bad, in my car. It's very hard to listen within when I'm multitasking. I take those rare moments when my cell phone, iPod, and radio are off to just rest while I eat. It's amazing all the helpful inner whispers I hear when I take time to slow down."

Envisioning and listening at the gym.

"Most people I know listen to some heavy pump-you-up music at the gym. I listen to meditation music and feel in the zone. I go to the gym for half an hour during my workday. Working out gets the cobwebs out of my brain, and I come up with wonderful ideas while running on the treadmill or practicing yoga. I also use part of this time visioning my intentions and praying. My belief is that the body is the temple of the soul. I hope it doesn't sound sacrilegious, but I feel so much more in tune with my spirit at the gym than I do when I go to church."

Meditate at work.

"My company has a meditation room. I go there for reflection and prayer as part of my lunch break. I come back to work feeling centered and relaxed. The answers to issues I was struggling with in the morning seem to be resolved during that brief time for contemplation. Even if your company doesn't have a special room, most folks can close the door to their office and hold the calls."

Change your location.

"If I can't actually get away from the office, I make a point of changing my location. It can often be as simple as switching from my desk to the couch in my office. I actually think of it as my 'inspiration couch.' The minor change helps me be receptive to new ideas as I listen within. I like to meditate on questions or issues I'm struggling with. Usually after five minutes, some answers have popped into my mind that weren't there moments ago."

Engage in a creative pursuit.

"I reserve time in our company conference room several times a week. It looks out onto a huge field filled with wildflowers. I use those occasions as my intuition time. I bring a notepad, colored pens and pencils, and do some creative mind mapping—which is a form of brainstorming. I get amazing results fast."

Choose peace.

"If I'm feeling really agitated and anxious, I bring to mind a line in the book *A Course in Miracles*. It says, 'I could choose peace instead of this.' I'll take a few deep, calming breaths and ask myself, 'How else could I be thinking about this?' or 'What would bring me peace in this situation?'"

Say a comforting phrase.

"I have a lot going on in my life and have to work hard to find peace in myself. Simple phrases or mantras are helpful in keeping me centered and connecting me to Spirit. My favorites are 'I am loved and protected,' 'I feel God's peace flowing through me now,' 'I am a child of God,' and 'Peace be with me and also with you.'"

Keep a photo of a wise person.

"I have three pictures I keep in my wallet. They are Jesus, the Dalai Lama, and my grandma (God rest her soul). They all represent people who are really wise and spiritual. When I feel like I need guidance, I pull out one of the photos and ask 'What would Grandma do?' or 'How would Buddha respond?' Usually an answer will pop into my head immediately."

Ask God.

"I feel that I have a personal relationship with God. I believe He exists in me and around me. I experience Him as a loving friend. I talk to him all the time saying things like, 'Is this the right action to take or the best way to respond?' Sometimes if I'm feeling discouraged I'll say things like, 'I'm feeling down right now. I don't know what to do. Please show me the right next step and the best attitude.' I just listen within. Sometimes the answers come quickly and at other times they'll arrive slowly or in a form I wasn't expecting. Asking the questions always centers me and makes me feel connected to a larger vision and purpose."

What are some ideas that might work for you? Think about your own style of listening. Be willing to experiment with some of the above methods. Mix and match them. Remember, this is your life, and you are an expert on you. Trust your intuition and discover for yourself the best way to hear your wisdom within.

God is working miracles through you so be still and listen. Surrender to His power and once you let go, the healing process will begin.
—LORI EBERHARDY

YOUR INTUITION JOURNAL

Think of an issue you've been struggling with. Write a few paragraphs about it in your journal.

Summarize the issue into a question. Some examples might be, "What's the next best step I should take regarding my career?" or "What could I do to improve my relationship with my husband?"

Once you have your question, close your eyes and turn within. Breathe deeply and evenly. Imagine you are retreating to somewhere peaceful and serene. This might be a beach, garden, ocean, mountain, or a specific favorite place you've visited. You can go there anytime you wish. When you find that centered place within, rest there for a few minutes.

Bring to mind your question and let it rest there. Allow the answer to come to you. It may present itself as an image, an inner voice, a fleeting impression, or an emotion. There are many ways you may receive the answer. When you feel ready, open your eyes and write down any answers you received.

Don't be discouraged if the information doesn't pop into your mind immediately. It may come later in the day when you least expect it.

Your Divine Connection is always on.

CHAPTER 3

Get in Sync with Your Instincts

You're the expert on you. While other people may be experts on how you're supposed to behave, only you know at a fundamental level what does (or doesn't) work for you.
—MICHAEL NEILL

You know you've made a bad decision. You had a sinking feeling when you were offered the job, but hey, you needed the money. The first week at work you realized you had Attila the Hun for a boss and knew you were going to have to keep looking for another job.

Or you felt a fleeting sense of anxiety as you walked out into the late-night parking lot by yourself. You thought, ever so briefly, of getting someone to walk with you, but dismissed the idea as silly. You ended up having your purse snatched with your money and all your credit cards inside.

Or you felt a nagging suspicion that your boyfriend of six months was lying about something. He assured you he loved you and that everything was great between you. You accepted that until you saw the recent romantic e-mail exchange between him and his "former" girlfriend.

You have wise guidance within you. It's your inner compass or GPS. It lets you know if you're about to take a bad job, steers you away from danger, and nudges you toward decisions that will result in success. When you're feeling good about something, that's your intuition saying, "Move in that direction."

It communicates through feelings, words, images, physical sensations, and dreams as well as through an inner voice. There's no one way that's the right way to receive this information. A fifteen-year-old girl defined her inner wisdom this way: "Intuition is when you know something, but, like, where did it come from?!"

One of the easiest ways to get in touch with your intuition is through your sense of enthusiasm. The word derives from the Greek root *entheos*. It literally means "God within." When you are doing something you're excited about, interested in, or energized by, you're following your guidance within. It's telling you, "Do more of this." It's leading you toward your success and best interests. Conversely, if you're feeling drained, bored, and anxious, that's also your intuition. This time it's telling you to pay attention, stop what you're doing, or move away from something.

Intuitive Messages Are Unique to You

Do you feel you "don't have intuition"? I believe all of us have it. I've never met anyone who either doesn't have it or can't develop it. You may have ignored it for such a long time that you no longer recognize it or trust it. Or you believe it should come in a specific form such as a gut feeling or unmistakable inner voice.

We each have our own distinctive ways to receive the information. It might be helpful to think back to a time you made a successful decision. How did you know it was the right one? Conversely, you've inevitably had times when you slapped yourself on your head and instead of saying, "I could have had a V8!" you said, "I should have trusted my gut!" How did your intuition communicate to you that you were heading in the wrong direction?

People who believe in trusting their intuition tend to be more successful in life. Oprah Winfrey, Microsoft's Bill Gates, and Virgin Airlines founder Richard Branson are all well-known gut trusters. It doesn't appear to matter how they receive this information. Inner wisdom may present itself through a good old-fashioned gut instinct, an inner voice, a fleeting sense of peace when the right answer arrives, or even through an angelic presence. Learn to pay attention to how you receive these impressions for yourself and check in with your inner intuitive success coach.

I've taught intuition development classes for twenty-plus years. In each class I ask people how they know they're receiving a "yes" from their intuition. Here are some of the responses:

- "I feel at peace."
- "My heart feels open and warm."
- "I hear an inner voice. It sounds different than the usual chatter that goes on in my mind."

- "I feel energized when I think of a decision."
- "I see what I call running videos as if they appear on a screen and I am watching them. They contain information that helps me make a decision."
- "It's a thought that stays with me. If it doesn't go away, I know it's intuition."
- "I feel safe."
- "I have a dream that shows me the right direction."
- "I just know."
- "An answer presents itself and it simply feels right."
- "A sense of calm comes over me, even if I'm making a difficult decision."
- "I feel like someone is wrapping me in a warm embrace."
- "I keep feeling nudged to make a certain decision. If I ignore it, the nudge becomes a shove!"
- "If I feel delighted, breezy, enlightened, invigorated, vibrant, elated, joyful, beautiful, then it is a good indication that I am doing what is right for me."
- "I get a tingling down my arms or up my spine."
- "Synchronicities begin to happen. I might hear a song on the radio or overhear a conversation and they'll help steer me in the right direction."
- "An idea pops into my mind that wasn't there moments ago."
- "When I close my eyes, the right answer seems to have a glow to it. It's as if it's saying, 'Pick me! Pick me!'"
- "It's like my inner GPS. It leads me in the right direction. If I don't pay attention, I can almost hear it say, 'Recalculating.'"
- "I close my eyes to access my inner wisdom. I'll see what appears to be a banner over the right choice or direction. It's as if it's saying choose me. It always steers me to success."

You can see from the above list that there are myriad ways to receive a yes response. You probably have a few that are unique to you.

Generally the way that intuition indicates a no or "don't go in that direction" response is the opposite of this list. You feel shut down, closed off, heavy, negative, irritable, depressed. You might perceive a negative image when you imagine making a decision your intuition is warning you against. Your stomach, head, or shoulders might hurt. One woman describes the no response from her intuition like this: "It feels like I just got a letter from the IRS that says I'm scheduled for an audit."

Think of a few of your past decisions. How did you know you were making a good or bad decision when you . . .

- Accepted your current job?
- Went on your latest vacation?
- Decided to get married (or not)?
- Ended a relationship?
- Decided to go to a particular school for your undergraduate degree?
- Chose your auto mechanic?
- Made a snap decision about someone?
- Changed your mind about a significant decision?

There are many more possibilities to add to the above list. Some of the answers may come to your mind immediately. Others may not. I'd like you to begin observing your decision-making style and make it more conscious. What feelings, images, physical sensations, and so forth go into your decision to say yes . . . or no to a particular option in front of you? How do you know you're right? Pay attention to how the decision turned out.

The Intuitive Decision-Making Exercise

Following is an exercise that I like to use when I'm making a big decision. There are no right or wrong answers. It's simply a way of accessing your inner wisdom. It's designed to circumvent your left brain, the side that demands logic and facts. That part of your brain may not have all the answers! Intuition comes through the vehicle of your imagination and is believed to be connected to the wisdom of your heart. Most likely you'll feel like you're making up your responses. That's the way it's supposed to feel. In other words, don't edit your responses. Let them come naturally.

1. Think about a decision you need to make. Perhaps you've been thinking about exploring a new career, beginning or ending a relationship, or moving to a new geographic area. For the purpose of this exercise, I'd like you to make a decision. "I choose . . ." Write down your full decision in your notebook.

2. As you write this decision, what's your immediate reaction? Do you feel relief? Excitement? Terror? Butterflies in your stomach? Be aware of all of your senses and list them in your notebook.

3. To help you concentrate, close your eyes and repeat the decision in your mind. What do you hear, feel, and think? Is there a physical sensation? Does an image come to mind? Perhaps you're aware of a scent or an inner whisper. Simply notice, without judgment, all your senses and jot them down.

4. Imagine telling someone about your decision. Who would you tell? What would you say? What's their reaction?

5. Did you tell someone whom you secretly thought would support your decision, or who would talk you out of it? Again, simply take note of your responses.

6. Imagine that it's exactly one year from now. Are you glad you made the decision? What's changed in your life? What's gotten better? Is there anything that hasn't worked out as you'd hoped?

7. It's now five years from now. What does your life look like? Has the decision you made today turned into a good one? Who are the people around you? What are they saying about your success?

8. Did you generally receive go-ahead messages from your intuition after completing this exercise? If so, what action step can you make today to make this decision a reality? Make the action step concrete and achievable.

9. After taking this action, did you feel good, happy, relieved? If so, you've made a great decision. Congratulations! Conversely, if

you felt depressed, overly fearful, or regretful, that's also a clue. It may mean you have to step back and reevaluate the decision. Either way, it's helpful information.

10. If you're still uncertain, you may want to try this exercise again making the opposite decision. Assess your results and determine which decision feels best to you.

Whenever you make any decision, especially a big one—marriage, divorce, career change, whether to have children, geographic moves, large financial purchases—it's normal to feel scared. We'll talk about fear and its relation to intuition later in the book. For now it's helpful to understand that you can feel the fear and do it anyway. Fear is not necessarily your intuition telling you not to do something. Entertain the possibility that it may simply be helping you move out of your comfort zone.

> There is a German proverb that says, "Begin to weave and God will give you the thread."

Something almost magical begins to occur when you make a major decision. A powerful energy is released from you into the Universe. You bring together your belief in yourself, your goals, your intuitions, your hopes, and your dreams into one big cosmic intention. It's as if you've said to the Universe, "This is what I want in my life. Help me make it happen!"

Your clear goal or intention, guided by your inner wisdom, sets off a chain reaction. There is a German proverb that says, "Begin to weave and God will give you the thread." When you decide and begin to take action—even a small step—the Universe is on your side, conspiring with you to bring about your dreams.

Good instincts usually tell you what to do
before your head has figured it out.
—MICHAEL BURKE

YOUR INTUITION JOURNAL

Think back to a time you made a successful decision and write about it in your journal. How did you know at the time that it was right?

What decision are you facing now? As you write about this, notice any answers that come quickly to you.

Is there an answer that makes you feel excited, interested, enthusiastic, relieved, and, yes, even a little uncomfortable? That's the one your intuition is encouraging you to take.

What small step(s) could you take today or this week to act on the wisdom you received?

CHAPTER 4

When Your Life Falls Apart

I try to listen for God's voice inside me, but my sense of discernment tends to be ever so slightly muddled. When God wants to get my attention, She clears Her throat a number of times, trying to get me to look up, or inward—and then if I don't pay attention, She rolls Her eyes, makes a low growling sound, and starts kicking me under the table with Her foot.
—ANNE LAMOTT

Like many of you reading this book, I've had times when my life has been upended. I'd like to tell you about one of those times. It's my hope that my tough time can help you find a path to successfully navigate yours.

I spent my early twenties working in a variety of nonprofit, social-service-type jobs. It was interesting and rewarding work. I felt pretty happy with my career choices, but most weeks I lived paycheck to paycheck. My savings account never had more than a few hundred dollars in it. When I did have any money, my car seemed to know about it and promptly broke down, necessitating an expensive repair.

When I was twenty-eight, I decided it was time to investigate the for-profit world. I diligently sent out résumés, went on interviews, and net-worked. Several months into this process, I heard about a job from a friend. It was for an executive assistant to a CEO for a start-up company. She told me about all the good things they intended to do in the world. It seemed like a perfect match for me. The job description was varied and interesting. Best of all, the pay was a 35 percent increase over what I'd been making in the nonprofit world. My friend put in a good word for me, I aced the interview, and a week later I was offered the job.

I was so excited! I would finally be able to have an apartment of my own, not one I shared with roommates. I could buy furniture. I could save up money to buy a newer car. The job required a move to upstate New York from where I'd been living in Boston. Some friends advanced me money as a loan against my first paycheck so I could put a deposit down on an apartment. I was on my way!

The first few weeks passed in a blur. I was busy with schedules, meetings, and setting up the new offices. The only downside was when my boss called me into his office and asked me to close the door. He told me that one of their investors had backed out. "Not to worry," he said, "Your paycheck will just be a little delayed."

I had been living on credit cards and a small amount of money I had left over from the loans. I figured I could hang on for another couple of weeks. I wasn't worried. The job was great, and the cumulative check I'd soon receive would put me back into good shape.

The Panic Begins

Unfortunately, it was not to be. The conversation with my boss was repeated several times over the next month. Each time with promises that "next week" this would all be settled. He even gave me $100 from his own wallet as a good-faith gesture.

After I'd been there for two months without a paycheck, he dealt the final blow. The company was closing. All the potential investors had backed out. There would be no paycheck. I was to collect my things and go home . . . but to where? To what?

I had no money. I had maxed out my credit cards to the tune of $7,000 (an enormous amount of money at the time). My rent was coming due again and I had no job and no friends in the area. I barely remember driving back to my apartment. I was sobbing so hard I had to pull over several times for fear I'd be in an accident. I didn't sleep that night. My mind was filled with nightmare images of being homeless, out on the street, begging for money.

The next week was filled with frantic attempts to find a job—any job. I filled out applications for fast-food places, for sales jobs, for temp jobs. Nothing panned out.

I'd always prided myself on my independence and self-sufficiency, but it was clear I needed help. I called a friend back in Boston and asked her if I could sleep on her couch until I landed back on my feet. To my immense relief she agreed. I loaded up my few things in a U-Haul, hitched it to my car—which was making ominous wheezing sounds—and headed back home.

During the day I would look for jobs. I was relatively calm because I felt I was taking action and doing what I could. But the nights were awful. I was experiencing panic attacks. It was something I'd never wish on my worst enemy. With each attack, I thought I was dying. If I managed to fall asleep, I'd wake up sobbing from nightmares. Unfortunately, my nightmare was my reality. My car had wheezed its last breath and I could no longer drive it. I had bill collectors threatening me, and my current roommates were making it clear they weren't too happy having a nonpaying guest sleeping in their living room.

I Receive an Answer

It was on one of those sleepless nights that I began praying. I had never been an especially religious person. Then again, I had never been that scared and that far out on the edge. I felt I had nothing left. It was at the end of a 3:00 a.m. crying jag that I remember praying, "Dear God, show me what to do!" I immediately felt a sense of peace around me. It was as if someone had embraced me with a warm and loving hug. Afterward, for the first time in three months, angst was replaced by peace, and as I was taking in this powerful new feeling I heard some words that spoke directly to my heart.

"You have abundance all around you. Ask for what you want."

In an instant I realized that my entire focus had been on my fears—what I didn't want. I didn't want to be in debt, sleeping on a couch, homeless, without a job, chased by bill collectors, unable to sleep. With that message, I knew I was being told to take the attention off my fears and focus it on faith. I also understood in that instant that there was abundance everywhere around me and that I'd been fixated—to the exclusion of all else—on lack. No wonder my life was upside down! I needed to turn my life around and head in a positive direction again.

I immediately sat down and wrote a list of what I wanted:

- A fun, secure, and well-paying job.
- Money for savings and to pay back my loans.
- A great apartment close to my work.
- New friends.
- A reliable, affordable car . . .

The list went on and on. I felt a sense of hope beginning to dawn. At the end of several pages, I closed my notebook and fell into a deep sleep.

At about ten o'clock that morning I received a call. It was from one of the places where I'd interviewed just outside Boston. They liked me. My skills were a match. Was it possible to start working with them this week?

Within a month of accepting the job, I found a small studio apartment that was within walking distance of my office. Within a year I had paid back all the loans from friends as well as the credit card debt. I had even started a savings account to put aside money for a newer car.

I learned so many lessons during that time. Most important—to pray, to stay focused in faith that good things would come forth, to ask for guidance, and to listen for the whisper of answers from the Divine.

Can I tell you that I have lived abundantly, experiencing no difficulties and full of faith for the rest of my life? I could, but I'd be lying. We all experience trying times. They often come when you least expect them. You get a frightening diagnosis from the doctor; your company has been bought and you're no longer needed; your spouse announces an affair; your kid is failing at school; you have to make some difficult decisions about an aging parent. We all go through these difficulties and hopefully come out the other side filled with a bit more wisdom, courage, compassion, and love.

When You're Broken Open

Elizabeth Lesser, co-founder of Omega Institute, the world's largest spiritual retreat center, wrote in her book *Broken Open: How Difficult Times Can Help Us Grow*, "Some of us need a cataclysmic event to find our way towards the center of our existence. Some of us don't. Some of us add up all of the smaller changes into one big lesson and find our way home as well."

I don't know whether my experience added up to what Lesser describes as a "cataclysmic event," although it certainly felt like that at the time. I do know that it was a life-changing event. It taught me to go within for answers to life's challenges. Key to this experience was the palpable and loving support I received from what I call God.

Early on in my work as an intuitive, I would feel terrible when something bad happened to someone. When clients came in who were sick, having relationship issues, or struggling with addiction, I would wish I had a magic wand to change them back to wholeness. While I still have enormous compassion for anyone who suffers, I've come to see that their struggles are often the very spot in their lives where they can allow God to enter and begin His healing.

Your Guidance Within

I believe that God is outside us and within us. We are part of Him as He is of us. He exists in the birth of a baby, the death of a loved one, the trees and the sky. Most importantly, perhaps, He exists and is with us in difficult times, guiding our path.

People often feel desperate about their situation and are willing to try anything to fix it. Finally, in defeat, they'll discover the wisdom to bring about true change. It's not always finding the perfect mate, winning the lottery, or achieving perfect health (although none of those can hurt!). It's knowing that at heart they are safe, they are guided, and that there is a kind, compassionate, and loving presence that resides within them and all around them.

If you're currently experiencing a difficult time in your life, sit back, close your eyes, and simply breathe. Be aware of the in and out of your breath for a few moments. Center yourself within.

Understand that from a limited human perspective you may not grasp why this difficulty is happening to you. The strategies that you've come up with on a conscious level may not be working. It's like you're seeing the picture of your life from the bottom of a large valley. You may feel lost and not know your way home.

Trust that there is a higher perspective that sees your life from the mountaintops, the sky, and beyond. It knows what's best for you and, like a GPS system, can navigate you back home to safety. It knows where you are and exactly where you need to go.

Receiving Answers

To become more receptive to intuitive messages, breathe in deeply and ask for wisdom with this simple question: "What do I need to know?" Listen. Be patient. Breathe. If the response gives you a sense of peace, you're receiving the right signal. Sit for a few moments more and when you feel ready, open your eyes. This is a wonderful all-purpose question to ask when you don't know the right question! "What do I need to know?" allows intuition to give you the information and direction you need.

You will find it helpful to write the answers as you receive them. Your Intuition Journal allows you to enlarge on the wisdom you receive—and it's nice to have a notebook filled with supportive and helpful information. You could also have received no perceptible information. Don't think too hard while you're doing this exercise. Intuition often communicates through whispers, small nudges, a felt sense, an almost imperceptible awareness.

If you're new to trusting your intuition, you may feel you received nothing and be disappointed. I believe that your inner wisdom is always trying to break through to communicate with you. Remember that as with any new skill, you have to practice to get good at it.

Intuition will also come when you least expect it—while driving to work, blow-drying your hair, washing the dishes, drifting off to sleep, or walking the dog. You'll experience an aha moment and find yourself with an idea that wasn't there previously. The information may not have come in deep meditation, but it's a communication from the wise part of your being. Honor it. Trust it. Take action on the knowledge and you'll be rewarded with more. It will begin to feel as natural as breathing.

The branches of your intelligence grow new leaves
in the wind of this listening.
—JALALUDDIN RUMI

YOUR INTUITION JOURNAL

Think of a challenging time you've gone through. As you write about it in your journal, ask: "How did I experience the presence of my inner wisdom?"

How can you apply what you learned to this current difficulty?

CHAPTER 5

The Transition Zone

Between letting go (of the old) and successfully launching the new there is a time of confusion and emptiness. People often feel lost during this time, and too often they interpret that lostness as yet another sign that something is wrong. It is simply a sign that they have entered the fertile chaos of the neutral zone.
—WILLIAM BRIDGES

It's downright scary going through a loss of any kind. If you've lost a job, you fear financial ruin, shame, loss of identity, your future. You may worry whether you can support yourself and your family. If you've lost a mate through death or divorce, you fear how life will be without that person, you wonder whether you will find love again. Life feels so full of unknowns.

At the level of everyday conversation, people are apt to tell you that everything is "great" even when their world is turning upside down. Unless you have close friends who are honest and open with you, you may not know that we all go through times like these. What makes these times especially painful is that we labor under the illusion that we are in the minority, the unlucky small percent who has had a run of bad luck. In truth, no one goes through life completely unscathed.

Many famous philosophers, poets, and teachers over the centuries have written eloquently about loss, pain, and the worry that accompanies life transitions. Here are but a few:

Success in the affairs of life often serves to hide one's abilities, whereas adversity frequently gives one an opportunity to discover them.
—ANCIENT ROMAN PHILOSOPHER HORACE

All misfortune is but a stepping-stone to fortune.
—American philosopher Henry David Thoreau

*The man of virtue makes the difficulty to be overcome his first
business, and success only a subsequent consideration.*
—Chinese philosopher Confucius

No one can avoid problems, not even saints or sages.
—Thirteenth-century Buddhist monk Nichiren Daishonin

*Even a happy life cannot be without a measure of darkness,
and the word happy would lose its meaning if it were
not balanced by sadness. It is far better to take things as
they come along with patience and equanimity.*
—Swiss psychologist Carl Jung

*Good fortune and bad are equally necessary to man,
to fit him to meet the contingencies of this life.*
—French proverb

The Limbo Period

Knowing you are not alone in your darkness may feel like a small consolation. Simply knowing there have been, and are, fellow travelers on your path doesn't stop the pain and fear. It's the "limbo land" between letting go of what you had and finding something new that is the hardest period to live through for most of us. It's the darkest time.

Danaan Parry, author of *The Essene Book of Days*, wrote an inspiring essay likening these limbo periods to a trapeze. "Sometimes I feel that my life is a series of trapeze swings. I'm either hanging on to a trapeze bar swinging along or, for a few moments in my life, I'm hurtling across the space between trapeze bars." He noted that our culture views the transition zone, what he calls the "space between bars," as simply a place of no importance.

He observed that this place is scary, confusing, and disorienting . . . a place we believe is a waste of time, to be gotten through as quickly as possible. Yet he went on to say that the transition zones are incredibly rich places that should be honored and savored. They're the places where the most growth and expansion take place. "It can be terrifying. It can also be enlightening, in the true sense of the word. Hurtling through the void, we just may learn to fly."

Marguerite was a client of mine who described a particularly painful life crisis. She and her husband, Joe, were one of those seemingly rare couples who were madly in love with each other after twenty-six years of marriage. It was a second marriage for both. They were in their late fifties, active, in great shape, and looking forward to an early retirement from their separate careers in the financial services industry. Unlike many who see their retirement years as a time for extended periods of television watching, Marguerite and Joe wanted to start a business.

They had always dreamed of working together. They wanted to combine their interests. Marguerite's dream was to work as a motivational speaker creating fun and interesting programs for young adults about the importance of money management. Joe had plans to become a CFP, a Certified Financial Planner. They felt it was a winning combination.

The dream started to become a reality when they rented an office, bought the office equipment, and began creating a Web site. They had an appointment one summer evening with the copywriter who was working on their marketing materials. The meeting was scheduled for 6:00 p.m., and at 6:30 Joe still hadn't arrived or called. Here's what Marguerite remembers:

It was unlike Joe to be late. He prided himself on punctuality. I got really worried because he wasn't answering his cell phone. I tried to go on with the meeting, but I was completely distracted with anxiety. At six forty-five the phone rang with his caller ID. I picked it up saying "Thank God! Joe! Where are you?"

A woman's voice answered. I will never forget her words as long as I live. "I have bad news for you, ma'am. We found your husband by the side of the road. It appears he had been out for a run and was hit by a car. I'm so sorry to tell you this on the phone. He died from the impact." I later learned that he was alive for long enough to give my phone number to a bystander who had helped him and called an ambulance.

In the days and months that followed, I was a wreck. My usual upbeat and positive outlook on life was replaced with depression, panic attacks, and sobbing spells that went on for so long they scared me. Friends came and went, bringing food, inviting me to dinner, and offering solace. Nothing seemed to break through the haze of fear and apprehension I was feeling.

I had spent the past twenty-six years with a man I adored, planning this wonderful future together. I had to come to terms with the fact that he was no longer here by my side and the future we had envisioned would not be the same without him.

Marguerite shared the above story with me on the one-year anniversary of Joe's death. She was still raw from the pain of his passing. However, she felt that she had reached a point where she could both honor her grief and sadness and begin to get back into the world to be of service to others. We decided to create an action plan of sorts to both recognize the transition period and take some baby steps to define life on her own terms as an individual with her own unique needs. Following are the ideas we discussed.

Honor Your Transition

What do you need right now?

Your needs and desires will change greatly over the course of a transition period. Focus on the current hour, day, or week and see if you can identify what you're lacking. What one small thing could you do to meet this need? The adage "Take it a day at a time" can be most true when you're experiencing a crisis. Marguerite reported that an hour at a time was all she could manage when she was overwhelmed with a flood of emotions.

Keep your sense of humor.

Marguerite told me she had a tendency to be a bit too serious and that Joe loved to make her laugh. After his passing she would find jokes popping into her mind at odd times. She decided that this was Joe's method of after-death communication. The thought comforted her and encouraged her to be on the lookout for life's small absurdities even amid the grief she was feeling.

Respect your suffering.

You need to be able to be with the pain you feel. Transitions bring up strong emotions such as anger, anguish, sadness, and loss. Honor them and know they are part of the healing process. A friend told Marguerite, "If you can feel it, you can heal it." This gave Marguerite permission to fully feel the times that sadness, grief, and anger overcame her. Allowing yourself to experience the so-called negative emotions also allows you to experience the joy, redemption, and happiness when you emerge from the transition period.

Acknowledge your vulnerability.

It takes a lot of energy to put up a false front of being "just fine" when you're not. Let people know you're hurting. Friends and family members often want to help but don't know how. Think about what would be helpful to you and tell them what you need. Marguerite said the weekends were especially tough for her. She asked people to include her in their plans where appropriate and not to assume she was busy with others.

Find meaning in your crisis.

This may be a good time to explore spirituality, religion, and philosophy. It helps to find depth and meaning when you're going through a difficult time. Marguerite discovered that biographies and autobiographies were valuable reading, as they showed her the lives of others who'd been through what she was going through. Reading these books can help you see that ups and downs, successes and failures, are a normal part of human existence. People (you) do go on to thrive and survive even after the most horrendous challenges.

Trust your inner voice.

Marguerite said that one of the difficult parts of losing Joe was being on the receiving end of well-meaning advice from others. "Start dating again!" "Join a support group!" "Take Prozac!" She found that true solace took place in listening to her own inner wisdom for direction. She designated a corner of her den as a place for prayer and meditation. She created an altar on a small round table. On it, she put fresh flowers, inspirational books, a shell that she and Joe had found on the beach while on vacation, a candle, a quartz crystal, and of course a photo of her and Joe. Whenever she felt the need for comfort, she would wrap a big cozy shawl around her shoulders, sit in her rocking chair, and ask for love, reassurance, and wisdom to be sent her way. "God delivered. I always left that chair feeling better than when I sat down."

Acknowledge your talents and interests.

When things get tough, we can find solace in hobbies, creative pursuits, and interests. Marguerite picked up a pastime she had learned as a child—needlepoint. "It was very meditative. I could focus on the patterns I was creating and not be consumed by my loss." Volunteering in a field of interest can also serve several purposes. You're out of the house and surrounded by others. You're being of service to someone else who needs help. It can also enable you to uncover a new talent or aptitude that may lead to a renewed sense of purpose.

Remember: This too shall pass.

Most likely you have gone through a life transition before. It could be a positive but anxiety-producing time such as graduating from college, getting a first job, or becoming a new parent. What helped you then? Each time you face a new challenge, remember to concentrate on the skills, talents, and resources that enabled you to survive the last rough patch. Marguerite knows that the pain of losing Joe will never go away—but it does diminish. There are ebbs and flows in life. She has been in a big ebb state for the past year. She's just beginning to welcome and embrace the new life that is waiting to emerge.

Marguerite called me again several months after her first appointment with me and reported that she had given a small workshop to a group of widows and widowers on the topic of financial planning for seniors. It was enthusiastically received, and she could feel Joe cheering her on from the other side.

When I'm in a transition zone myself and fear that nothing is moving forward, I find comfort in the example of tulips. You plant them in the fall, and they come up in the spring. In the intervening months there appears to be nothing going on. You wouldn't think of digging them up in the middle of winter and yelling at them that they're "stuck" and admonishing them to "grow faster!" They are doing exactly what they need to do. And when all the circumstances needed for their flowering are right, they appear and bloom. The same is true for your transitions. The wisdom that guides the flowers guides your life as well. Choose to trust it and have faith. All will be well.

Darkness is not the whole of the story—every pilgrimage has passages of loveliness and joy—but it is the part of the story most often left untold. When we finally escape the darkness and stumble into the light, it is tempting to tell others that our hope never flags, to deny those long nights we spent cowering in fear.

—PARKER J. PALMER

YOUR INTUITION JOURNAL

Honor the transitions, however painful they may be. They are meant to help you heal and point you in a new direction. You're being prepared for something you cannot yet see.

If you're going through a particularly painful time, meditation and quieting the mind are very helpful. Instead of asking "What's wrong with me?" try the following technique:

Close your eyes. Take a few deep breaths and find the place of calm within yourself. When you feel ready, say one or more of the following statements:

"I want to feel calm and at peace."

"I am open to new possibilities."

"Life is taking me on a wonderful new path."

"Everything I'm experiencing is helping me."

After you've made these statements silently in your mind—wait. See what intuitive communication emerges. You're simply allowing the space for your inner voice to make itself known. Write about the insights you've received.

CHAPTER 6

What You Say to Yourself Matters

Do not anticipate trouble, or worry about what
may never happen. Keep in the sunlight.
—BENJAMIN FRANKLIN

Alex is an architect. He was in my office several months ago for a session. He is ordinarily a handsome man, very well dressed, with a slight European accent. Unfortunately, this day he looked like the picture of gloom when he began telling me of a business relationship that had gone sour. He painted a dreadful picture of a once successful business doomed by mistrust, miscommunication, and deception. "Nothing works anymore. I can't get clients. I feel like I'm in prison because of this situation."

I think Alex could have filled the hour with this discouraging tale if I hadn't stopped him. I was beginning to feel depressed! I asked him what I thought was a simple question. "What would your business look like if it was successful right now?" Alex paused for a moment and then went right back to telling me how dismal things were and would likely continue to be in the future.

Think Like a Visionary

Fortunately, I had a flash of intuitive insight, and I tried a different tack. "Alex, you're an architect. Your clients come to you when they have a vision for a new home, an office complex, or a rehab of an existing building. They see the completion of their project in their mind's eye. They see a beautiful building that will be the headquarters for a successful business. Or they see a magnificent home that will house their growing family.

"You take their vision, add your own elements of magic through your architectural and design skills, and create a thing of beauty. The important thing is that both you and your client have to hold a vision of the end result in order to create the successful finished product.

"What if a potential client came to you and said, 'I don't know what kind of building I want. I'm not even sure what kind of business I'm creating or where I want to put it. The business probably won't be successful because every other business I've been in has failed. In fact, I'm not sure I have enough money to pay you.' It doesn't take impressive psychic perception to know that this client is going to fail. In fact, you would probably kick the client out the door! Well, right now you're thinking and acting just like this bad client."

I could tell that what I said had hit home. He looked a bit startled and then nodded. "You're right," he said. "I've been my own worst enemy. How do I begin to turn this around?"

Alex and I worked on a plan. He was to begin writing down what he wanted to happen in his business. If he were to be successful, what would it look like in six months? A year? He loved designing and drawing things. He said it helped him to visualize, so he sketched pictures of his success. This included things like seeing a proposal he submitted with "hired" stamped on it. He created a mock magazine cover emblazoned with the words "award-winning architect" along with his picture. He used PhotoShop software to produce a very real-looking photo of himself standing in front of a huge building. His client was handing him a check for a large amount of money, made out to Alex's company.

Break the Pessimistic Thought Habit

The tough part for Alex was shifting his habitually negative thinking. It didn't stop overnight. He told me that he had quit smoking years before. "I realized my thinking patterns were simply a pattern I had to break. When I was smoking, I would often find that I had a cigarette in my mouth and was about to light it without even being consciously aware that I had shaken the cigarette out of the box.

"With my negative thinking, I had to become aware of my thoughts, catch myself, and shift the thought in a new direction. At first it was very hard. It required a lot of effort, but I knew the payoff would far outweigh the effort."

I had Alex write down his most frequent negative thoughts to see if we could find a new statement, an antidote of sorts, to help shift him to a more positive direction. I wanted this exercise to be grounded in reality. I wasn't looking for simple affirmations. For example, I didn't want Alex's statements to shift from "I'm on the verge of bankruptcy" to "Millions of dollars are now flowing to me easily." I knew that wouldn't be a believable thought.

Alex admitted that he occasionally had some moments throughout the day when he actually felt good. When he was in a more optimistic frame of mind, I asked him to counter his usual negative messages with something more positive. I wanted him to check out whether his habitual statements were really true.

I gave him a series of questions to ask himself about each of his negative statements:

- Is this negative thought really true?
- Would I say this statement to a good friend? If not, why do I keep repeating it to myself?
- What thought feels better?

Here's a sample of some of what Alex and I came up with:

Negative Thoughts	Positive Thoughts
I'm such a failure at business.	That's not true. I've actually accomplished many positive things in my business. I even have some major awards from my peers in the architecture field.
I may go bankrupt.	My financial situation is only temporary. I have made it through tough times before. It's very likely I'll make it through again. With a few new projects, I can turn this difficulty around.

I'm getting too old for this business.	I have the respect of my clients because of my years in this business. My employees like working with me because I'm good at teaching them things.
I can't seem to get new clients.	I'm creating a step-by-step plan to reestablish contact with clients I've worked with before and asking for both new business and referrals. This has a high chance of success.
I feel so alone.	I'm working with a coach. I'm also joining some professional organizations. This will help me feel reconnected to people.

Alex worked on these statements and the actions involved for several months. He meditated daily, continued to visualize, and began to feel more connected to the world around him. He called recently to report that he had just been awarded a highly sought-after project and his firm was on the short list of finalists for a big state contract.

Being Your Own Best Friend

It occurred to me after speaking with Alex that we often block out the wise messages from our intuition through our habitual thinking.

Have you ever had a friend who was going through a tough time and was incredibly negative about her situation? When you're together, she constantly harps on her difficulties and wails that it will never get better. "There are no good men out there!" "The economy is so bad. I'll never get a job." "You just can't make a good living anymore." "Other people seem to have all the luck, not me!"

As her friend, you may have some very wise and insightful words and ideas that could truly help her. Unfortunately, she is so focused on her pessimistic way of thinking that she's not open to hearing what you have to say. Your words—"Have you tried this?" "I have a good idea," or "Perhaps you could think about it this way"—simply fall on deaf ears.

It's the same thing with hearing your own inner wisdom. It's there to be your friend and to guide you to the right next step. It wants you to be successful. It wants to help you find your dream job, a terrific mate, a way to make more money, or whatever your heart desires. However, in order to steer you correctly, you need to open your mind to receive its guidance.

The Negative Messages We Give Ourselves

Many of us have negative thoughts. They're messages we constantly repeat to ourselves so often we begin to believe they're true. I had a colleague who was a fellow speaker. She was incredibly funny, energetic, and outgoing. If she mispronounced a word, lost her train of thought, or misunderstood something that someone said, she'd get very animated, make her fingers into an L-shape, hold them up to her forehead, and proclaim, "I'm such a loser!"

I thought it was just part of her act until I had a more personal conversation with her one day. The L-word kept coming up in our chat over coffee. "Marilyn, you don't really believe that about yourself, do you? You're so successful. I really admire you!" I guess I shouldn't have been surprised when her eyes welled up with tears. She admitted that she often compared herself unfavorably with others. She felt that she never really measured up to her own high standards and did, in fact, feel like a loser.

I saw her a few months later, and she recounted our conversation. She said, "When you asked me about those 'loser' comments, I realized it was something I said to myself quite frequently. I had to have a long hard talk with my own inner self. I knew it wasn't really true and I needed to shift my self-talk. Thank you for pointing it out. I want to be a positive role model for audiences, and that wasn't a constructive thing to be doing for them or me!"

Molly also used self-talk as a means of change. She was a client I hadn't seen for several years. I remembered her as having lots of energy. She was very focused and ambitious in her financial services career. She had an appointment with me recently, and I didn't recognize her at first. She had been in a car accident and was in constant pain. She told me that for months after the accident she felt terribly depressed.

My mind was just filled with negative thoughts. Thoughts like, "I'll never get better. I'm in so much pain. I'll never work again." It was all too easy to be focused on worry and pain. One morning I was just lying in bed feeling overwhelmed by everything and I heard a little inner voice. It said, "Change your thinking and change your life."

It's funny with those intuitive messages. It can be something very simple, like the message I heard, but the words seem to come packaged with a lot of information. When I heard that phrase in my head I immediately recognized that what had helped me create success in business was the very thing that could help me to heal my body and feel well again. I had attained a lot of success in my career by constantly motivating myself with positive self-talk.

I hadn't thought of applying this to my healing. At first I felt like Stuart Smalley, the comedian in that Saturday Night Live skit. He was the one who made fun of affirmations by saying, "I'm good enough, I'm smart enough, and, doggone it, people like me!" That made me laugh, so it wasn't all bad! But I had to create something that worked for me and my situation.

Instead of saying, "I'm in so much pain!" I replaced it with, "Today I'll feel as good as possible." When I felt panicked that I'd never be able to work again, I told myself, "I'll get through this and it will all work out." When I felt scared I'd never be able to resume my career, I'd say, "God has a plan for me and I know it's a good one."

Molly shared with me that she felt the accident had been a blessing. It had slowed her down, put her in touch with her spiritual side, allowed her to make time for friends, and brought her closer to her husband. Her pain was beginning to lessen and she said, "I feel so much stronger, centered, and whole."

Like Marilyn and Molly, you may not even be aware of the negative messages you're giving yourself. The ones I hear most frequently are: "I'll never get ahead," "I'm stupid," "I don't have what it takes," "I never do anything right," "I always screw up relationships," "I'll never make any money."

Building Positive Self-Talk

What strategies can you create that will begin to change negative thinking patterns? Here are some tips:

- Keep a notebook with you for a few days. Write down your most frequent negative thoughts.
- When you're in a good mood, begin to counter some of those thoughts with positive ones. Write them down! You may want to ask a good friend, coach, or therapist to help you with this.
- When you're in a bad mood, look at your good-mood responses!
- Be gentle with yourself. Isn't it the height of absurdity to hate and do battle with your own inner critic? "I just had a negative thought. Out! Out, damn thought!"
- Do something fun to switch the channel on negativity. Take a walk. Call a friend. Rent a funny movie. Go out to dinner. Go bowling. Watch people. Read a good book. Try something new.
- Don't take yourself or the situation too seriously. Things have a way of changing for the better.
- Answer the question, "What does my life [or this situation] look like when it's successful?"
- Build your self-esteem by taking a risk, something that requires a little courage. Acknowledge and reward yourself for doing it.

Sometimes all that's standing between you and the great life you want and deserve are a few negative beliefs and perceptions. When you feel insecure and inadequate, begin to see it as a message from your own Spirit that you're thinking too small. Your inner wisdom is challenging you to try new things and move in creative directions and is simply showing you where change is needed. It's a wonderful world waiting for you. Have courage and embrace the change. Mighty forces gather around you and whisper words of encouragement. Open your mind and listen.

> *The remarkable thing is we have a choice every day regarding the attitude we will embrace for that day. I am convinced that life is 10% what happens to me and 90% how I react to it. And so it is with you. We are in charge of our attitudes.*
>
> —CHARLES SWINDOLL

YOUR INTUITION JOURNAL

What negative statements or phrases do you habitually use? Begin to catch yourself and turn them around to something more positive.

In your journal write down several of these negative statements. You may recognize some from the examples in this chapter. Take about five minutes for this.

Your intuition has a message that allows you to shift your self-talk in a more positive direction. Close your eyes. Take a deep breath. What message are you receiving right now? When you feel ready, open your eyes and write down the answers you receive.

CHAPTER 7

Your Recipe for Miracles

*Live each day as if you expect a miracle. You are your miracle!
Your power tools are imagination, thinking and desires, and
your precision instruments are intuition and illumination.
Imagine God's glory pouring through you, and make it
bold enough to pay dividends.*
—EDNA LISTER

Lisa is a client who first called me when she was in the midst of a very big life transition. She was recently divorced and a single mom to eight-year-old Jack. She had received her certificate to be a nutritionist and was struggling to create a fledging business to support herself and her son. She had used the small settlement she received from the divorce to put a down payment on a ranch house near her parents that she and Jack lived in. Her ex-husband had lost his job and wasn't maintaining regular child support payments.

At our first appointment Lisa was in a panic. She had spent the previous two months going from one specialist to another trying to figure out the source of Jack's skin rash and headaches. The consensus was he had a chemical sensitivity to something in the house Lisa had just purchased. She had spent her business start-up money on doctor's bills as well as construction costs related to making the house less allergenic for Jack. She was down to her last $500, and there were no new clients in sight.

Lisa was scared she'd have to sell the house. If she did that, she feared it would uproot Jack from his new school and cancel all her efforts at creating her business, leaving her without a support system and perhaps leaving them homeless.

I often hear people report that they feel like life has a way of getting out of control when they're going through a big change. Lisa said, "I feel like I'm drowning. I'm out there in the water and no one is throwing me a lifeline." As I listened to her describe her life situation, she was filled with pessimistic predictions and fears. "What will happen if I can't sell the house?" she'd tell me, or "I worry that if I don't get more clients, we may have to live with my parents or be homeless and then it will be even worse."

After a few minutes of listening to Lisa, I stopped her and asked her to take a deep breath, close her eyes, and affirm to herself that she did, in fact, have what it takes to get out of this situation. This was a temporary situation made worse by her "awfulizing" about her predicament.

I wanted to help Lisa shift gears and focus on more positive outcomes. Since she was a nutritionist and I love to cook, I shared with her my idea that food preparation is a lot like life. If you put in a bunch of bad ingredients (negative thinking), you're going to end up with an unappetizing result.

It's human nature to worry at least a little. However, in order for positive change to occur, you need to shift your thinking and change your ingredients! I love what the book *A Course in Miracles* says: "Miracles are natural. When they do not occur, something has gone wrong." I thought Lisa could use some miracle thinking to help her turn around her situation. I told her about my six-ingredient recipe for miracles:

1. Keep Your Focus on the Positive

When life is challenging, it's all too easy to think about how bad things are. You might even imagine and spend time dwelling upon how these bad times could get worse and how your life will become really difficult. It's important to understand that your thoughts, beliefs, and emotions have power. The fear, panic, and anxiety you feel are often the result of the habitual thoughts in your mind.

What can you do to turn these around? "Out of difficulties grow miracles," said French author Jean de La Bruyère. Begin to think about what you would like to happen. Esther Hicks has a great sentence completion exercise that I love. "Wouldn't it be great if . . ." You fill in the blank with whatever your heart desires. Grab a pad of paper and complete as many of those sentences as you can think of.

Here are some examples that Lisa came up with. Wouldn't it be great if . . .

- "A wonderful part-time nutrition job came my way that would pay benefits."
- "Jack would get better and we could stay in our home."
- "New clients would come to me easily and effortlessly."
- "I made some great new friends in the neighborhood with children who were Jack's age."
- "I could have $10,000 or more in my savings account again."

It might take you some focus and practice to break the habit of habitual worrying, but the dividends will be huge. Because of your new openness, your intuition will be able to deliver some brilliant new ideas. You'll also be receptive to synchronicities and coincidences that will open up new possibilities and directions.

2. Use the Power of Your Mind

After you've gotten clear what you want to happen, don't try to figure out how it's going to happen. That's for the Universe to resolve. It's part of expecting miracles. An element of faithful expectation is involved. Picture the desired outcome that you want. Take the statements you wrote and begin to imagine and feel them as vividly as you can. Spend time each day visualizing what your life will look like when this imagined situation is created.

Lisa's visualization involved seeing herself working part-time for an organization as a nutritionist. She liked the idea of having the structure and security of a job while she established her own business. She imagined Jack healthy and happy with neighborhood kids to play with. She saw other moms enjoying tea at her house while they watched the children. She visualized people calling for nutrition appointments and saw her appointment book filled each week.

Every morning and evening she put on some relaxing music and let her imagination play with the above scenarios.

3. Surrender and Accept

When you're in the midst of a difficult situation, it's extremely hard to imagine a way out. Many of the spiritual traditions recommend releasing or surrendering the problem to Infinite Intelligence. You are asking the Power that grows the trees, creates the sky, and makes the sun rise every day to create a miracle just for you.

Acceptance means that you let go of struggling as best you can and accept that things are the way they are for right now. We all hold a picture of what our lives should look like. We'd be in a happy relationship, our bodies would be healthy, our families would be loving, we'd be productively employed, and money would flow in. You get the idea!

When you are in acceptance mode, you're letting go of your expectations about how you think your life should be and simply acknowledging and appreciating what is. Any thoughts you have such as, "It shouldn't be this way!" or "What am I doing wrong?" create more tension and frustration. You may not understand why things are the way they are, but acceptance puts you in the Divine flow of life.

In effect, you're changing your words to "I may not understand why this is happening to me right now, but I'm accepting that all will be well and all is well." You're trusting that a Divine presence is working behind the scenes. God is in control of each and every day, bringing about healing, opportunities, and miracles. You might as well relax and try to enjoy the unfolding. Your job is to listen to your intuition and take action on the information you receive.

Here's an exercise that will help you shift into acceptance mode. Sit in a quiet place and close your eyes. Briefly envision your current situation. Use whatever words fit your belief system to ask for help. For example: "I ask for your Divine wisdom and guidance in this situation. Please guide my thoughts and actions. I invite and welcome your help to create a perfect outcome for all involved. I release this to you, in faith, with the knowledge that all is well."

4. Invite Miracles

Much has been written about the power of gratitude. You may find it help-ful to add daily moments of gratitude to your Intuition Journal. When you're feeling thankful, you open up to the energy that invites miracles. For example, you're out of work and you're afraid you won't be able to pay the mortgage this month. Each morning when you wake up and before you go to bed at night, close your eyes, go within, and affirm, "Thank you for the mortgage payment." Or, simply, "I am open and receptive to money flowing into my life. I know that abundance is my true nature. Thank you." When you're scared and worried, make a conscious decision to open your heart and mind to whatever it is that you want. Anticipate and say thank you as if you already have it.

When Lisa did this, she became more aware of the fact that she had a great deal to be grateful for. In her prayer she expressed appreciation for her nutrition degree, that Jack seemed to be getting better, that she lived in a nice neighborhood, that she was healthy, and that life was offering her possibilities. She ended with thanks and faith that new sources of abun-dance were on their way to her.

5. Dwell on Optimistic Expectation

Have you ever been around someone who is a complainer or fearmonger? It's draining! "The gas prices are awful." "The economy is going down the tubes." It's basically what Lisa was doing with her catastrophic thinking about her home, work, and Jack's health.

If you find yourself thinking like this, shift your focus. What you say to yourself is often a self-fulfilling prophecy. It may take some work to change your habitual thoughts, but it's worth the effort. Try saying things like, "Let me be open to new ideas." "Things have a way of working out for me." "The economy may be bad, but I'm open and receptive to new avenues of income." "I've gotten through tough times before." "I trust my inner wisdom to guide me to a better situation."

6. Listen Within

Your intuition is your inner compass. It points you in the right direction. If you're feeling down, scared, and worried, that's your intuition inviting you to shift your focus. It's telling you to choose thoughts and actions that will make you feel better. If listening to your intuition feels difficult, or if you're out of practice, try this: Each day choose one thing you commit to doing that makes you feel better. It could be as simple as changing an habitual negative thought, taking a walk, hanging out with positive people, not watching the news. Intuition guides you toward miracles and lets you know which direction will produce the success you seek. It communicates through images, words, dreams, feelings, and physical sensations.

Lisa met with me again about eight months after our initial session. She reported that she had felt an urge to call a man she had done some training with as part of her nutrition degree. He laughed at the synchronicity of her call. He had been planning to call her. He was going on a yearlong sabbatical and thought she would be perfect to work with his clients while he was away.

Her ex-husband had moved to be closer to her and Jack. He had become positively involved in his son's life. He had found a job and was paying regular child support again.

Her nutrition background helped her land a part-time job as an instructor at a weight loss clinic. She enjoyed her co-workers and often got together with them socially.

Jack's health was almost back to normal. The source of the problem had been narrowed down to mold in the walls of his bedroom. Repairs were made, and his headaches and rashes were now rare. He loved his new neighborhood and had lots of new friends.

The Reverend Robert H. Schuller said in one of his sermons, "Impossible situations can become possible miracles." Miracles happen every day. You can create them in your life. Let your thoughts be open to possibilities. God wants you to succeed. He is constantly sending messages to encourage your receptivity to His miracles. Your life can take a turn for the better in a moment. I've seen it happen so many times, and I know it can happen for you.

Thank you, God, for the ideas You place in my mind and heart.
I am open and receptive to embrace the visions You would
have me manifest. I let go of my adopted limits and open
myself to be a vessel through which great ideas, love, and
healing can come to life. Within me now are the answers to
all my questions. I trust You to give me the power and the
means to accomplish any idea you would have me manifest.
I go forth with a mighty confidence that all the good
I seek is available and already done.
—ALAN COHEN

YOUR INTUITION JOURNAL

In your journal, write the words, "What miracle am I seeking?"

As you begin writing, become aware of the pictures that form in your mind. If you're having difficulty imagining this, here are some questions to get you started:

- What does the outcome look and feel like? Who are you with?

- Where are you living? What kind of work are you doing?

- What do your supportive friends and family members say about this wonderful change in your life?

Begin to hold a vision of the outcome you seek. Keep your heart and mind steady on this idea. Ask for guidance that will draw this situation toward you. Act on the wisdom you receive.

CHAPTER 8

Managing a Noisy Mind

*We are not responsible for every thought that goes
wandering through our mind. We are, however,
responsible for the ones we hold there.*
—PETER MCWILLIAMS

To most people I appear to be a fairly calm, centered person. I would have
to agree . . . with one exception. It's when I meditate. I try to focus on the
gentle in-and-out of my breath. But you wouldn't believe the things I have
rocking and rolling in my head. It's like a bunch of hyperactive cats in
there. Despite this, I meditate twice a day for at least fifteen minutes at a
time. Why? Because usually at the end of the meditation those crazy cats
are purring and I actually feel calmer, more connected, and at peace.

On a bad day this is what it looks like:

Sit. Close eyes. Focus on breath.

*Should I take the shrimp out of the freezer for supper? Or
maybe we can go out for Chinese. I've been wanting to try that
new restaurant down by . . . Oh right . . . I'm supposed to be
meditating.*

Breathe . . . Breathe

*I should really get to that PowerPoint presentation today. Did
I remember to ask my assistant to send my books to the conference
location? Oh right! I'm meditating.*

Breathe . . . Breathe . . . Breathe

*I wonder if some people sit down to meditate and immediately
go into a blissful altered state? I wish I could do that. I wonder
if I'm doing something wrong? No. All my meditation teachers
say to notice my thoughts and just bring my attention back to my
breath. Be gentle with my agitated mind. I should have done some*

laundry this morning. What am I going to wear tonight? Oh right.
I'm meditating. Be gentle. Slip back into watching my breath.

Breathe . . . Breathe . . . Breathe . . . Breathe

Oh hey! I'm doing pretty well with this watching-my-breath
thing. I'm catching on to this. I know that it's not the point to just
be focused on the breath. It's about being gentle with myself, going
within, staying present, focused. Being calm. I'm pretty calm right
now, aren't I? Good. This is great! I'm great! Wow! . . .

I wonder if I fell asleep? What time is it? Oh . . . darn! I've
only been meditating for three minutes. It feels like a long time.
Oh! An e-mail message! I got an e-mail! I wonder if it's from
my editor. I hope she likes my latest chapters. Meditate. Breathe.
Yeah. Right. I'm really good at this. No judgments. Focus. Notice.
Just breathe. Bring my attention back to my breath.

Breathe . . . Breathe . . . Breathe . . . Breathe . . . Breathe . . .
Breathe . . . Breathe . . . Breathe

You get the idea! I just re-read what I wrote. I feel like I've flunked
meditation and I'm admitting it to the whole world. It's even hard to believe
that I actually get pleasure and benefit from something that sounds so crazy,
but I do. There are moments of sublime connection when I feel wonderful,
connected to All-That-Is, and the world is full of possibility and love. I live
for those times and wish I could conjure them at a moment's notice. I find
that when I take the time to slow down, even with my mind racing, it's time
I'm spending with God.

Sometimes all I can manage is sitting still for ten minutes and saying,
"God, I feel so busy and overwhelmed today. Please enter my mind, heart,
spirit, and life and imbue me with your peace. Thank you."

Even though I obviously struggle with it, I consider meditation one of
the best tools for listening within and connecting with the Divine Presence.
I desire a close relationship with God, so I want to spend time with Him.
Think about it another way—if you want to have a good relationship with
your spouse, mate, partner, you'd want to hang out with him; you'd want
to communicate and let her know she's important to you. Meditation is one
of the ways we keep in contact with God.

Benefits of Meditation

Meditation is free and it requires no extensive training, special equipment, or purchases other than what you'd commonly find in your own home. It's been around for thousands of years. There's a large body of scientific evidence proving that meditation helps improve our physical functioning. It's been shown to:

- Reduce stress
- Improve sleep
- Relieve anxiety
- Boost energy
- Improve memory
- Heighten immunity
- Increase alertness
- Reduce pain

Meditation can be invaluable when you're experiencing a challenging time in your life (or even when you're not!). I simply find that it improves my intuition, and helps me feel less alone and part of a larger cosmos that supports and encourages me. You can't buy all of the above in a pill.

Ways to Make Meditation Easier

Not having enough time is the biggest issue I hear from people looking to begin the practice of meditation. Why not start when you're already in bed in the morning? Set the alarm fifteen to thirty minutes earlier, then sit up in bed, pile some pillows under and around you, and begin your day with meditation. It's a great way to start the day. I find I'm much more centered and efficient doing this practice first thing. I also find I don't have quite so many distractions on my mind.

At the end of my meditation time, I'll spend at least a few moments envisioning how I want my day to go. I'll see a seminar that I'm leading and imagine it going well. I'll visualize the new business meeting at lunch and see it resulting in a sale for more training and intuitive work. Everything just seems to flow better when I start this way. I'm more in the flow of coincidence and synchronicity. I meet the right people at the right time and opportunities come my way.

Creating a sacred space is important for some people. I love the idea. It can be as grand as a large, ornate room or as simple as a comfortable chair with a candle next to it. Do something to make it special. Maybe add some colorful pillows, a pretty rug, some flowers, or personal sacred objects that represent a loved one or some aspect of your faith or religion.

I have a friend who lives in a tiny apartment in New York City. She keeps her meditation space in a drawer! When she wants to practice her meditation, she brings out from the drawer a pillow, a candle, a statue of Buddha, a photograph of her family, and some incense that smells wonderful. Voilà: instant meditation room!

Another friend, who has three kids, is blessed with large walk-in closets. She's cleared a corner of one of them and set up a unique meditation room for herself. She puts a sign on the closet door that says "Mommy meditating. Do not disturb unless there's an emergency." This worked well for her until she overheard her youngest child say very politely to a neighbor who had rung the doorbell, "My mommy is home. But she's in the closet with Jesus." There was some explaining to do after that.

Find a Way That Works for You

There are many different kinds of meditation. There's no one way that's the right way. You just have to find what works for you. In larger cities there are always meditation classes and teachers. You can also find a lot of resources on the Internet. Simply type in "how to meditate" and you'll come up with lots of options and more in-depth information than what I've provided below. Information can also be found in books on the topic and CDs with guided meditations. One of my favorite sources for guided meditations is my fellow intuition author Belleruth Naparstek. Her site is www.healthjourneys.com.

The basic idea behind meditation is to quiet your mind. The meditation I practice and am most familiar with is a simple Mindfulness Meditation. Choose a time to meditate when you know you'll have ten to thirty undisturbed minutes. Some people do this with their eyes partially open. I prefer to close my eyes. Sit upright with your back straight and simply focus on your breathing. Feel your breath come through your nostrils and slowly fill your chest and abdomen.

No matter what kind of thoughts come up—and they will—simply say to yourself, "I'm letting that thought go for right now. I'm simply focused on my breath slowly moving in and out of my body." Meditation teaches us gentleness and an ability to forgive ourselves and to move on. The focus is on one breath at a time.

I like the gentleness of it. I try to not berate myself for losing my focus. Some days are better than others. My intention is to be gentle. I allow the distracting thoughts to float by as if in a stream.

At first I felt that I was "doing nothing" and that it was either a huge waste of time or I wasn't doing it right. However, after only a few days, I began to experience all of the aforementioned benefits. The main ones were that I slept better, had less anxiety, was much more positive, felt more connected to my purpose, and had more energy. It was enough to make me a convert!

After I practiced this for a while, I found that I developed what I think of as a "mental muscle" that allows me to bring my thoughts back to my breath. Each time I have a distracting thought and can pull back into the present moment with my focus on breath, I'm making that muscle stronger. In my daily life I catch the beginnings of worry, anxiety, and negative thinking and find it much easier to bring my thoughts back into alignment with peace.

Other Ways to Meditate

Sit in a garden or some other quiet place in nature and use all your senses. Be in the present moment. Notice the birdsong . . . hear a car passing . . . feel the breeze on your skin . . . watch the clouds . . . smell the scent of flowers wafting through the air. Don't forget your sixth sense—your intuition—and listen within.

Try some mindful physical activities. I find this helpful if I'm especially agitated about something. Sitting and meditating when I'm in this state simply doesn't work for me. I like to go for a walk or a swim. My objective is to quiet my mind by putting my focus on the activity, trying to stay in the present moment, shifting my focus away from my restless thoughts. Other people love yoga, running, surfing, and dancing.

Choose a mantra—a word or phrase that calms you. Some common ones in English are "I am," "Peace, be still," "I surrender to your will," "All is well," and "I am open to what is." As you meditate, focus on your mantra and bring your attention back to it when your mind wanders.

You might also find some Sanskrit words helpful in this type of meditation. Here are a few that are often used:

- OM—the sound of the Universe
- Sat Nam—truth
- Om Namah Shivaya—transformation
- Shanti, Shanti, Shanti—peace, peace, peace

One of my favorite Buddhist meditations is called "lovingkindness." Simply repeat the words: "May I be filled with lovingkindness. May I be well. May I be peaceful and at ease. May I be happy." You can also change it to "May you be filled with lovingkindness," and so on, if you want to direct it to another person.

Other classical phrases include, "May I live in safety. May I be healthy. May I live with ease." If you are extremely upset and worried, these are all wonderful phrases to repeat to yourself. They're very centering and calming.

If all else fails, put on some lovely meditation music. The calming tones will soothe your soul. My favorite artists are Max Highstein, Steven Halpern, and Riley Lee.

A meditation can be anything that takes you into silence. Try it next time you're in line at the grocery store, or waiting at the doctor's office. You don't have to close your eyes. Simply notice your surroundings and your breath. Stay in the present moment and send love to yourself and others. Remember to listen.

You can have everything if you let yourself be.
—Donovan Leitch

YOUR INTUITION JOURNAL

Spend a few moments in silence at the beginning of the day. It's a helpful way to enhance your ability to listen to your intuition.

Think about the intentions you've written about in the previous chapters. Ask questions of your intuition that relate to your intentions.

For example: "What could I do today to be more at peace?" "What is my intention or purpose today?" "What could I do today to attract more abundance?" "What could I do today to find work?" Make up your own according to your situation and needs.

Don't be discouraged if the response from your intuition doesn't come immediately. Be alert for the answers to come at different times throughout the day. They may arrive when you least expect them!

CHAPTER 9

Breaking the Worry Habit

*I believe God is managing affairs and that He doesn't
need any advice from me. With God in charge, I believe
everything will work out for the best in the end.
So what is there to worry about?*
—HENRY FORD

There is a question on my "Life Transitions" survey that asks, "Is there anything you wish you had done differently to help you through your time of crisis?" Almost 40 percent of respondents checked the box that said, "Worried less." Time after time people wrote about coming out of a difficult period feeling more resilient, stronger, and more confident. What would have made their time in the dreaded transition zone easier? Trusting more and worrying less. "I worried about the future so much that it became my present nightmare," lamented one woman.

Another woman wrote, "The worst part of this crisis was the sleepless nights I spent worrying. I worried about whether I was going to end up a bag lady in a homeless shelter, whether anyone would ever love me again, whether I'd have a job again, whether God had forgotten me. I was only forty-five years old and felt my world had ended when my husband asked for a divorce. I wish the 'future me' could have spoken to the frightened, anxious woman I was then and reassured me I was going to be okay. Today, five years later, I'm happy and confident. I've been dating a wonderful man for the past eight months. I have a job that feels like it was made for me, and I have a whole host of terrific friends. I didn't think I would ever say this, but the divorce turned out to be one of the best things that happened to me. I just wish I hadn't spent so much time worrying. I was my own worst enemy!"

Let's be honest and admit that worrying seems to be human nature. We all do it to one degree or another. Some people who are chronic worriers feel that it gives them a sense of control over the future. If this bad thing happens, they reason, then they'll be prepared! However, a recent study in the journal *Clinical Psychology & Psychotherapy* found that 85 percent of the things we worry about never actually occur.

What is worry exactly? I think of it as making up stories in our mind. They're usually self-talk narratives filled with dire pictures of what we fear will become of our situation or us. Author Corrie

"Worry," said the Hopi Indian Grandfather David, "is like praying for your worst fears to happen."

ten Boom wrote, "Worry does not empty tomorrow of sorrow—it empties today of strength."

When you worry, you create an energy vibration of fear that is not conducive to attracting the life you want and deserve. "Worry," said the Hopi Indian Grandfather David, "is like praying for your worst fears to happen."

Switch the Channel on Worry

Worry is like any bad habit. It can be addictive. One small fear leads to another and another. Before you know it, you've imagined your life falling apart, not only now, but ad infinitum into your future. One of the ways to begin breaking any habit is to simply recognize you're doing it! "Oops— there I caught myself imagining not being able to pay my grocery bill again."

But simply recognizing that you're worrying isn't usually enough to change it. What can you do to switch the channel? Ask yourself the question, "What do I want?" For example, if your worry du jour is imagining yourself broke and penniless, turn it around. What you probably want is to feel safe. You might also want to imagine having enough or more than enough money. Your task at this point is not to figure out how this will happen, it's simply to begin choosing something you want versus something you don't.

Sometimes you don't know what you want. Or the thought of imagining something so dramatically different stops you in your tracks. If this

> **If you can't sleep, then get up and do something instead of lying there and worrying. It's the worry that gets you, not the loss of sleep.**

is the case, switching the channel on worry may be to simply say, "I want to feel at peace," "I'm choosing not to worry right now," or "I'm open to something easier."

If you've got a bad worry habit going on, you may need to be patient as you retrain your brain. Also, all of this is much easier at three in the afternoon than at three in the morning when you're lying awake without a lot to distract you! The great positive thinker Dale Carnegie once said, "If you can't sleep, then get up and do something instead of lying there and worrying. It's the worry that gets you, not the loss of sleep."

Keep Your Focus on Gratitude

You've gone through a loss—a job, a spouse, a way of life. You're probably overwhelmed with shock, pain, and grief. It's hard to imagine life can turn around again. However, you must find a way to keep joy alive even during this difficult time. What are you grateful for? Do you have a friend you can count on? Give her a call. Do you have happy memories you can recall? Create a scrapbook. Is there a piece of music that makes you happy? Keep it with you on your iPod. Find those small, soul-sustaining slices of pleasure and plan to experience them throughout your day.

Pray for Peace and Guidance

Prayer works. It's one of the things that survey respondents mentioned most often. If you don't know what to pray for, simply ask the Divine to bring you peace, to help you to feel calm. "God, I welcome your love. I invite your peace. Fill my heart and soul with your wisdom. Show me my next steps. Give me courage and hope. Sustain me with your message."

You may wish for a direct, clear message from God. Sometimes that happens. More often, you'll feel a sense of peace that wasn't there before, or you'll be drawn to a passage in a book that provides comfort.

Pay attention to that "still, quiet inner voice." It's one of the ways that the Divine imparts His wisdom.

Distract Yourself

If you find yourself at the bottom of a huge worry pit and can't dig yourself out, distract yourself for a while. Put on some music and dance. I love the "Three Little Birds" song by reggae musician Bob Marley. The main line is "Don't worry about a thing, 'cause every little thing gonna be all right." Get your favorite feel-good music lined up and ready for those occasions when you feel particularly down.

Sitting alone and thinking about your problems only serves to intensify them and make you more miserable. If all of this spiritual, feel-good advice isn't making you feel better, get out and do something for someone else. Check out a homeless shelter, a soup kitchen, a day care that could use some volunteers—anything that temporarily gets you out of your house and circumstances. Sometimes all you need is to feel less alone and join the human race again.

The cartoonist Charles Schulz was reported to have said, "Sometimes I lie awake at night and I ask 'Where have I gone wrong?' Then a voice says to me, 'This is going to take more than one night.'" If you're like Mr. Schulz, you may want to keep a pile of things that can distract you when you wake up in the middle of the night. This is the worst time for most of us when we're going through a tough time. At 3:00 a.m. it often seems like a long time until the light comes up and the world feels friendly again.

Distraction items can be a sudoku or crossword puzzle, a good novel or audio book, meditation music on your iPod, a craft project, a card game, a funny movie, or something like the American Idol series on DVD. If you're up for it, clean out a drawer, a box, start on your garage. It's amazing what you can get done when you need a distraction!

Stop Worry Overdrive

Joan was laid off from a job she'd held for twelve years. It was her first job out of college. She had been promoted up through the ranks and had imagined she would stay with the company until she retired.

The people I worked with were like family to me. I was totally devastated when my boss called me into his office and told me they were closing my department. I hadn't seen it coming. I think I had been in denial. My whole life was my work. I not only lost my livelihood in a down economy, I also lost my social life. I was given a two-month severance package and some outplacement counseling.

For a while I was just in shock and not really responding to my situation. I just caught up on errands, organized my house, and did some yard work. I kind of felt I was on vacation. Then it just hit me one day about a month after the layoff . . . what the heck was I doing?

I went into worry overdrive. I worried about everything! I felt so out of control. Would anyone hire me again? What if I needed to go back to college? What if I had to move? What if I had to borrow money? What if I couldn't pay the rent? Each what-if came complete with awful images of me being down and out and desperate. I became rather emotionally paralyzed for a few months. My severance had ended and my meager savings were running out.

If you buy the theory that what you focus on with your thoughts and beliefs is manifested in your life, why not put all your attention on what makes you happy, challenged, and healthy? One of the techniques that works for many clients when they're feeling upset is simply to ask themselves, "Is there another way to think about this issue/concern/worry?" They begin to catch themselves in the early stages of worry and negative thinking and begin to focus on what they want instead of what they don't want. That's a powerful point of change in stopping the process of worry.

Focus on What's Working

You can't hold two thoughts at the exact same time. When you hold attitudes of gratitude, you'll find serenity returning and the worry disappearing. Our culture has been very invested in focusing on "what's wrong." For instance, when was the last time you heard of massive research funding for studying healthy, happy people? When was the last time you went to a therapist who asked, "What makes you happy?"

Have you ever gone to a doctor who congratulated you on all the things that were working well in your body? There's power in the attitude of gratitude and positive focus. It's a potent tool for directing your life and releasing your worry and anxiety. It may be that your kids are healthy or the fact that you have nice neighbors. What's working in your life? Begin to focus on that.

Set Aside Worry Time

Give yourself ten minutes a day and only ten minutes to really worry about something. Get into all the worst-case scenarios that could possibly occur. Write about your worries and elaborate on them. If you find your anxious thoughts beginning to occur at any other time during the day, tell yourself you'll focus on them only during your allotted "worry time."

One day at a time has become the motto of many recovery programs. Do what you can with today, and tomorrow will take care of itself. When you've experienced a crushing loss, you may find yourself being able to take it only an hour at a time. Do what you need to do to get through your day. A caveat: If getting through your day regularly includes drinking, drugs, or some other addictive behavior, it's time to seek out help.

Intuition Interlude

Next time you catch yourself fraught with anxiety and upset about the subject of your worry, check in with your intuition. Get in the habit of asking questions of your intuition and expecting a reply. You might ask, "What could I do to feel calmer about this issue?" In response, you get an image of a quiet lunch in the park by your office. That's one of the ways your intuition responds—through images. Your intuition is connected to a higher wisdom that knows what you need. It will always lead you to peace, forgiveness, and gratitude.

If you have fear, worry, or anxiety about anything,
recognize that those feelings aren't from God because
He has promised to give you a spirit of power, love, and
a sound mind. There is tremendous power in peace.
When you are at peace internally, you can think
more clearly. You can hear the voice of God more easily.
You'll make better decisions.

—JOEL OSTEEN

YOUR INTUITION JOURNAL

Finding a strategy to reduce worrying is easier when you're not in the grip of anxiety.

Choose a moment when you feel relatively calm today. Pick up your journal and write out some strategies. Look at some of the suggestions in this chapter. Which ones resonate with you? What are some ways for you to connect with the Universe in order to feel calmer? List at least three things you can do when worry begins to overtake you.

CHAPTER 10

Life Is What You Make It

There is no way it is. There's only the way you say it is.
The Universe hasn't made up its mind about you.
It only knows what you show it today. You are the Inventor.
Your life is the Invention. You get to make it up.
So make it up good.
—GAIL BLANKE

I was standing in line for the roller coaster with my then ten-year-old step-son. I don't like roller coasters. They scare the heck out of me. Cliff was determined to ride one, and I was determined he wasn't going alone. We got in the little cart. The bars closed down to seal us into our seats. Please God don't let us fall out! I gripped the handlebars for dear life. I noticed Cliff had a big grin on his face.

The cart started to rise slowly as the people behind us took their seats. I was praying fervently. Cliff laughed delightedly, whooped with joy, and began gesturing at the sights all around us as we began to move higher. I was feeling nauseous, and we'd barely left the ground.

I glanced around me and noticed a number of people grimacing, crying, eyes closed tight, looking like they wished for all the world that the roller coaster would stop before it hit the top and began to free fall. One woman was clearly mouthing the words "Oh no!" and "please God." Her knuckles were literally white.

The other group was already wildly cheering, smiling, arms out-stretched, ready to experience the event for all it was worth. "Wahoo!" "All right!" "Let's go!" Which group was right? Were roller coasters a horrible, scary ride or were they fun, exhilarating, and exciting? Clearly there were two opposing beliefs with this group of riders!

As we started up the first steep slope, it suddenly struck me. Being on a roller coaster is a lot like life. You always have ups, downs, and neutral zones. It's just the way you experience it that determines whether you have a lovely journey or a dreadful one. I realized I had a choice. It was in that moment I decided I was going to join Cliff in having fun on this ride. I released my death grip on the bar in front of me and threw up my arms just as he did. Wow! What a rush!

Looking back with many years of hindsight, I remember that day at the park with crystal clarity. It was a huge amount of fun. I don't remember being scared, only the thrill of being in the air, having a great experience with Cliff, and overcoming my fear.

Nurturing Beneficial Beliefs

All of us hold different beliefs about and have different reactions to life events. To one person a job loss can mean that life as she knows it is over. To another it can be an exciting challenge and an opportunity for more money and adventure. One person can experience a divorce as a death of sorts. Another person can sign the divorce decree and feel he's been given a new chance at life.

Which beliefs are right? Neither? Both? The real questions to ask yourself when you're going through a tough time are, "Which beliefs help me? Which ones hinder me?" There isn't an all-purpose right answer here. You get to choose! In the 1960s a popular poster read, "When life hands you lemons, make lemonade." When you shift your negative beliefs toward more positive ones, you're making lemonade.

You Can Change Your Beliefs

You may not be able to choose the circumstances of your life, but you absolutely can choose your reaction and response to them. If you're finding yourself increasingly disheartened by your current life situation, pay attention to what you're telling yourself. If your self-talk is a constant chatter of things like, "My life is over," "Nothing good ever happens to me," "I'll never get through this," "I always screw up," and so on, and so forth, you'll continue to feel miserable. You have a choice of how you view these events. The beliefs you hold are changeable. It may take some practice.

You may also have to be vigilant to catch yourself frequently as you begin to change these thoughts.

In my twenties I took a class in metaphysics. The teacher, Robert, was an accomplished and well-known musician. He expected a lot from his students of music and metaphysics. He deeply disliked it when anyone said something self-defeating or negative. If you dared to utter thoughts like, "It's hard to make a living at this," or "That's not the way the world works," Robert would stop everything he was doing, look you squarely in the eye, and state, "If you say so!"

I hated it when he said that to me! I have to confess, all these many years later, that he was very effective at getting me to be more positive. I can scarcely have a negative thought without hearing Robert's voice challenging any defeatist attitude.

Change Your Focus

Last year I worked with a business coach for several months during a rough time in my business. Similar to Robert, she challenged me to change a particular "story" I was telling myself about why my business wasn't working. Doing the following exercise gave me insight into how I could change that inner narrative and move on to something more productive.

- Describe your current life circumstance.
- Write down eight things abut this experience that really upset you.
- What's a different way of looking at this experience that makes you feel better?

I found the technique so helpful that I recently suggested it to my client Jane, who had just lost her job. Here's an abbreviated version of what she came up with:

> I'm terrified I won't find a new job. The economy is really bad. I didn't go to college so no one will hire me. I've only had one job so I'm not qualified for anything else. Maybe I'm too old for a new job. I don't have a lot of skills. I'll run out of money. What if I end up in some dead-end job that I really hate?

I would never have left this job of my own accord. However, I was really bored with it. Maybe there is a much more exciting one coming my way. Even though I had one job at my last company, I actually did a lot of different tasks. I could put those responsibilities on my résumé and expand my options. I have a little money in savings and could do some odd jobs to tide me over until I get a "real" job. It will actually be nice to have a little downtime to do some house projects I've meant to do for a long time. Ninety-five percent of people are employed in my region of the country. That means there are jobs out there! Even though I didn't go to college, I could take some courses that would add to my skills.

If you look at Jane's words in the first paragraph, you'd probably feel as depressed as she was. There's no way out. No job. No prospects. Nothing good.

In the second paragraph the situation hasn't changed—just Jane's response to it. Which frame of mind do you think is more conducive to Jane receiving some helpful inner wisdom? The things she's saying to herself in the second paragraph will attract coincidence, synchronicity, and luck because she's more open to guidance.

Intuitive Guidance Can Change Your Life

I'd like to share the story of Carmel, one of the people who responded to my "Life Transitions" survey. She was depressed, recently divorced, and mom to a seven-year-old son, Cooper. Her intuition led her step by step out of a situation where she felt hopeless about her future into creating a fabulous organization helping other single moms. Here's her story . . .

Life can be difficult sometimes. But for me, in the months imme-diately after my divorce, it felt downright terrifying. It was like watching the world pass by with the sound tuned way down. Soci-ety clearly went about its business but I didn't, not really.

Yes, I was functional. I brushed my teeth and did the laundry and somehow picked up the groceries, but I was never aware of doing any of these things while I was doing them. Sometimes I'd reach into the fridge for milk and wonder how it got there. Or I'd suddenly notice that I was miles out on the freeway and had forgotten where I was going in the first place.

I worried about how my post-divorce blue period was perceived by my young son, Cooper. He was only seven, but what did he make of Mama somnambulating around like a lost ghost stopping only to hug him, holding on for dear life, for solace?

The haze and paralysis were quickly chased away by the cold reality of economics. After seventeen years in a happy, prosperous marriage, I suddenly found myself plagued by worry and doubt. How on earth was I going to support this little boy on my own? Fear gripped me by the throat . . . a deep, relentless sense of doom pervaded everything I did or felt. And it wasn't just about money; it was the loneliness, it was not understanding my place in the world anymore, not knowing where I now belonged.

For the first time in my adult life, I felt utterly powerless and alone. At nights I'd wait for Cooper to fall asleep and then curl up in a fetal position crying . . . not on my own comfy bed in my own, beautiful house, but on a stranger's bed in a small room that I was forced to rent upon relocating to Los Angeles after the divorce. I knew I had to shift my thinking, find a new way of looking at life, and take action. I just didn't know where to begin.

For a while I allowed the fear to take over. The worry about where I could go and what I could do infected every waking moment. The sensation became so gut wrenching that I retreated into meditation. I had begun this practice many years before and found that it would bring me peace.

It was in a prolonged meditation that I had a realization . . . a warm peaceful feeling filled my body and mind. A clear intuitive thought pierced the fog. It was filled with peace, joy, but mostly with pure intention. It told me to "find another single mother to share with."

Bolstered by this clear message, I went in search of a house big enough for two families. When I found the house, I posted *a notice: single mom seeks same to pool resources and share a house with a garden. Let's work together to create a safe environment for our children. I received eighteen responses.*

At first I felt that the "something good" that was happening was all about me. But as I started to have conversations with the moms who responded, it became clear that this was bigger than me. This was about all of these women looking for a way to connect, and not just for house sharing, but as single mothers who needed to reach out to someone who understood what they were going through. But I only had one house . . . what could I say to the other seventeen?

After chatting with several of the moms over coffee, it struck me that some might have more in common with one another than they had with me. Two had three-year-old boys. One mother had a sixteen-year-old girl and lived close by and another had a fourteen-year-old girl. It made perfect sense to put them in contact with each other. And so I did. And they were grateful. If eighteen single moms were looking to share with another single mom in my small neighborhood, how many hundreds must there be in the Greater Los Angeles area? How many thousands in California? How many millions in the United States?

I did some research and found that there was no forum where single moms could find each other to house-share. That familiar intuitive feeling came over me . . . and I was listening . . . Why not me? Why not take the initiative and create my own vision of a place for us single moms to connect, a place for us, by us, where we can pool resources to build healthier, happier, more secure home environments.

Carmel ultimately founded a Web site, CoAbode.org. It's designed exclusively to connect single moms for house sharing and friendships. Today she has 20,000 members, thousands of whom are sharing homes together all over the United States. Her organization has been featured in *Time* magazine and *USA Today*. She's been interviewed for books, and has been a guest on television talking about her innovative idea. It can take just a moment to make the shift from depressed and hopeless to finding that one idea that can change your life (and many others) forever. Carmel found it through listening to her inner voice.

Obstacles are those frightful things you see when you take your eyes off your goals.
—HANNAH MORE

YOUR INTUITION JOURNAL

Is there a negative belief you hold? Perhaps it's a repetitive thought that makes you feel bad. Observe your thinking this week. If you find yourself feeling anxious, angry, hopeless, or some other strong negative emotion, check in with yourself. What were you dwelling on just before this feeling began?

In your journal draw a line in the center of the page. On the left side write the negative beliefs. In the right column answer the question, "What belief would make me feel better?" Listen for the answer.

CHAPTER 11

The Uneven Path to Success

*Faith is belief in the unseen, the quietly held conviction
that even though you can't imagine how, at some time,
in some place, in the right way, the thing you desire
will indeed come to pass.*
—DAPHNE ROSE KINGMA

"When am I going to get through this?" wailed Sally when I spoke with her in my office. "I've been praying, saying affirmations, and visualizing like crazy and I still don't have a job!" It's something I hear on a regular basis. When you desperately want something to happen, it never seems to come fast enough.

Is there a secret to achieving huge results quickly? Can I speed up my success? Is there a lesson to be learned before a goal is accomplished? Why does it seem like manifestation and the Law of Attraction are working for everyone else except me?

In my ideal world you would receive a small box at the beginning of a crisis, neatly tied with a bow. Inside, it would have three pieces of information:

1. Here is the lesson you are meant to learn by going through this particular life challenge.

2. Here's what you could do to make this time in your life easier.

3. Here is the end date to your current crisis.

Details would follow each of the above. For example, after number 3 it might read: "On May 15 of this year, you will . . . have a wonderful job . . . meet your soul mate . . . experience a miracle healing . . . win the lottery . . . successfully end your court case . . . achieve enlightenment . . . fill in the blank!"

Why Is It Taking So Long?

Oh, if only life were so easy! How do you wait? What do you do when your life is on hold . . . seemingly forever? Like Sally, you may feel like you've been set adrift on a vast ocean, praying for rescue and yet still not seeing signs of land or help. Every one of us has gone through times when progress appears to stall, stop, or even go backward. Yes, even the people who have achieved great success. It doesn't mean you are doing something wrong. It's also not a "sign from above" that you are destined for failure or on the wrong track.

The honest truth is that setbacks, disappointments, and outright failure are often part of the bumpy path to achieving success. These crises challenge our way of thinking. They get us to try new things, to look at life in a whole new way, and to gain strength in our weak areas. Life disasters test everything about us but can ultimately build courage, inner wisdom, faith, and integrity, as well as clarity about our dreams and intentions.

Notice Your Persistent Thoughts

If you're like most of us, it's difficult to wrest your thoughts away from your current misfortune. It may be your rapidly dwindling bank account, a job loss, a spouse's infidelity, a health challenge with your child, or any combination of situations that threaten your hard-won peace of mind. You simply find yourself scared, aggravated, and anxious. Your mind is filled with negative thoughts like "I'll never be good enough," "Things don't work out for me," "I must be doing something wrong," or "I'll never get out of debt."

You may recognize the fact that thoughts like the above simply breed more counterproductive thoughts and feelings. You're putting your focus on what isn't working. The Law of Attraction states that we attract life circumstances based on what we're predominantly feeling and thinking. Let's take the statement "Things don't work out for me." When that persistent thought runs through your head, all you can see is evidence that supports it. "I got overlooked for a promotion at work. I didn't get a raise. My son is getting a C in math at school. My husband is coming home late. My car needs repairs . . ." Stop! It's clearly time to shift your thinking!

When you think negative thoughts, you attract more negative thoughts, negative people, negative experiences, negative results, and yet more negative thoughts. Who needs that? Certainly not you or anyone else who wants to turn their life around and create success, peace, joy, abundance, love, or any other wonderful situation!

So what can you do when you find the external circumstances of your life seemingly not going in the right direction? Start to put the focus on what is working. Even in the midst of crisis there are moments of joy. Here's the big secret to turning life around: Begin to notice the good, wonderful, surprising, and precious things that are currently happening in your life.

Shift Your Thinking

How do you do that? Let's take our friend Sally, who is concerned that her prayers for a job are not being answered quickly enough. Her work experience was in public relations. When I listened to her talk about her day, it was a litany of complaints. "The traffic was awful on the way to that job interview and I know I wasn't even considered for the job because I was late." And "I went on four interviews at the same company last month and they didn't even have the courtesy to tell me they gave the job to someone else." She added, "The economy is so awful. Everyone with my skill set is getting laid off, so I probably won't even find work in my field."

Nothing was going Sally's way. I listened to her complain and rant for about ten minutes. Simultaneously, I was checking in with my own intuition about how I could be of assistance to her. I knew that she was blocking her own inner wisdom, which was seeking to show her some new avenues for abundance and success. I suspected her negativity was overriding all the positive inner wisdom her intuition was trying to provide.

Finally, I held up my hand and said, "Sally, what good things are happening in your life right now?" She stopped suddenly and stared at me as her eyes welled up with tears. She spoke slowly, "I'm a single parent. I have a son who is nine and I just adore him. He's the love of my life. This period of unemployment has allowed me to spend more time with him. He's doing better in school. The teachers have noticed a huge improvement. He's making friends and seems to feel more at ease with himself. I wish I could get a job with a flexible schedule so I could be there for him even more."

"Pushing Against" Versus "Allowing"

Sally continued talking about what she was grateful for and what she really wanted in a job. It became apparent to both of us that finding another high-pressure public relations job would not be ideal at this time in her life. As she softened while talking about her son, she spoke about having a desire to be self-employed, to make her own hours and work from home.

I could see and feel the energy shift as she talked about this idea. Feelings of enthusiasm, relief, excitement, and interest are ways that intuition communicates. Sally was exhibiting all of these. "What's stopping you from doing this?" I asked. She started to sputter about the bad economy, layoffs, you-name-it, and then caught herself. She said, "There isn't anything in my way. In fact, a small company I interviewed with last month asked me if I'd be willing to work on a freelance basis instead of full-time. I guess I just wasn't open to the idea. I could start there and take some strategic action to add a few more clients. This could work!"

I heard from Sally a few months later. She reported that she was handling the public relations for two small companies on a freelance basis and was about to add a third one. I loved what she said: "I look back at those months of unemployment as a gift. It was horrible and painful to go through, but I've come out the other side with enough joy and stability to make it all worth it. I realized I had been taking a lot of action toward something I really didn't want—the high-pressure job. The pain of that experience really forced me to go beyond my comfort zone. It gave me permission to do something I've always wanted to do. If I hadn't been forced to the wall, I may not have taken the risk. I'm not making as much money as I was, but I know things will get better. For both me and my son, I'm glad that it all worked out. Life is a pleasure now."

You may feel like a trapeze artist in these "in-between" times. You've let go of one bar and find yourself hurtling through space hoping to catch the next bar, where you can hopefully rest safely for a while. The space between is often filled with fear, anxiety, and desperation. Will you get to reach that next bar safely? What can you do when your own life is in this natural, yet uneasy place?

Cultivate patience.
It's common for most of us to underestimate how long it will take to reach a goal. You may think of the period between your old life and the new one as simply a time of interminable waiting. It may feel that way, but it's still your life. Eckhart Tolle, author of the book *The Power of Now*, wrote, "Realize deeply that the present moment is all you ever have." What can you do to enjoy and be fully present at this moment in your life?

Keep an evidence log.
Your goals, wishes, and desires are not usually presented to you all at once. They show themselves by arriving as small successes, synchronicities, and a general feeling that things are going your way. An evidence log is similar to a gratitude journal. Writing in it is a wonderful way to direct your focus to the positive things in your life. Begin each day with a few things you're grateful for, and end each night with notes to yourself about what went right.

Take daily positive action.
Creating a big change in your life can be downright overwhelming. Where do you begin? This is the biggest hurdle for most of us. Don't give up on your dream because the path from here (where you are) to there (where you want to be) seems too daunting. Commit to taking at least one action each day that will lead you in the direction you want to go. Ask your intuition, "What could I do today that will help me _____?" Fill in the blank with your current goal. Pay attention to any thoughts or ideas that feel interesting, fun, or have some energy to them. Then take those steps!

Imagine you've already succeeded.

One of the best manifestation tools I use is to see my life as if I already have what I want. Years ago I had the dream of being a published author. I sat in my chair every morning and saw myself as having succeeded. In my mind I would visualize myself holding a copy of my book and silently saying things like, "This book is beautiful. I'm so grateful that I've been able to write it and have it published. I love receiving notes and e-mails from people who have been touched by my words. I'm thankful that this book allows me to expand my speaking and consulting business. I appreciate all the many opportunities that come my way to promote this book and show others the power of their inner wisdom." The book you're reading is my seventh book. I like this technique because it works!

What would you be saying to yourself a year from now if you're thriving, successful, and flourishing? Some people like to record these statements. Others find it effective to imagine friends, relatives, and colleagues congratulating them on their success. You can also write notes to yourself acknowledging your victories. Play with this. It's meant to be fun and not tedious. It can be a wonderful way to acknowledge your greatness while you're on the sometime uneven path to success.

Being with the way things are calls for an expansion of ourselves. We start from what is, not from what should be. We encompass contradictions, painful feelings, fears, and imaginings, and—without fleeing, blaming, or attempting correction—we learn to soar, like the far-seeing hawk, over the whole landscape. The practice of being with the way things are allows us to alight in a place of openness, where "the truth" readies us for the next step, and the sky opens up.

—ROSAMUND STONE ZANDER AND BENJAMIN ZANDER

YOUR INTUITION JOURNAL

Take two minutes to write about a time when you failed at something.

When you've completed that, take ten minutes to write about how that "failure" ultimately opened new doors to opportunities, helped you learn something new, or gave you a different perspective.

The honest truth is that setbacks, disappointments, and outright failure are often part of the bumpy path to achieving success. Honor them, accept them, and know that your inner wisdom is continuing to guide you to safety and the happiness you seek.

CHAPTER 12

Take the Next Right Step

The road to happiness lies in two simple principles: Find what it is that interests you and that you can do well, and when you find it, put your whole soul into it—every bit of energy and ambition and natural ability you have.
—JOHN D. ROCKEFELLER III

One of the more difficult things about going through a huge change is that you often feel directionless. It's also at these times when you feel unable to mount a big campaign to get clear about your goals and take action.

Misguided loved ones may encourage you to "get over it," "let it go" or "buck up" and proceed with your life. If it were only that easy. Your old life is gone, and you probably feel you don't have a clue about where you're heading. Even if you did, you may not know how to get there.

Depending on your circumstances, you could be feeling depressed, hopeless, tired, overwhelmed, or all of the above. None of these emotions puts you in the optimistic mood necessary to create the positive change you so desperately want or need. However, I love this irreverent quote by Lee Iacocca: "So what do we do? Anything. Something. So long as we just don't sit there. If we screw it up, start over. Try something else. If we wait until we've satisfied all the uncertainties, it may be too late."

You're Not Lost. You're Exploring!

It's also a bit like looking at a map for directions when you're unclear about your destination. It's hard to get there when you don't know where "there" is! My dear friend Jana Stanfield, a songwriter, has a wonderful song titled *I'm Not Lost. I'm Exploring*. One of the lines is "I have joy as my compass and faith as my map."

Greg described how he felt after his wife asked him for a divorce. He also wrote about the immediate aftermath:

I was just shell-shocked when Sarah announced she wanted a divorce. We had been going through a tough time financially. I had taken on a second job so Sarah could stay home with our three-year-old son, Ben. I know I wasn't around a lot and wasn't being the dad I wanted to be to Ben. I just figured we were a family and that working more to make ends meet was a temporary thing. When we got out of debt, I could go back to one job and I could have family time again.

I guess Sarah saw it differently. She didn't see us as close and thought the situation with my not being around would never change. I have to admit we didn't talk about this much. I feel very guilty about that even now. She simply announced one morning that she was going to stay at her mom's for a while "for support." I thought it was for a week or so, but she basically never came back except to pack up her things and move out.

A year later we were officially divorced and I was seeing Ben only every other weekend. This was never what I had imagined when we got married. I thought we'd be married for a long and loving life and have more kids. I was just so depressed that I could barely get myself dressed and out to work. I wasn't eating or sleeping well. I didn't have any close friends, just a bunch of "buddies" who claimed I was lucky to "be free."

After many months of feeling like I was in a free fall, I woke up one morning and remembered a dream I'd had the night before. I couldn't recall the details, but three words kept ringing in my head. They were, "Just one step." When I thought of this, I felt like there was an inner voice encouraging me to do one step each day to feel better.

I had been incredibly overwhelmed by the loss of my wife, my son, and life as I knew it. I hadn't been able to shake the depression I'd fallen into. However, "just one step" was something I thought I could manage. I sat there drinking my morning coffee and thought about what the "one step" could be today. The only thing that popped into my mind was to walk. I had read that exercise helps you feel better. So I walked around my little neighborhood before *taking off for work. People said hi to me. The day was beautiful. I had to admit, I felt a little better after doing that.*

I got into a habit. Every day I would wake up and ask myself, "What's one step I could take that would make me feel better?" Sometimes they were little things: sending a card to Ben, making myself a nourishing meal, buying flowers for my kitchen table. Sometimes they were bigger things: joining a men's group at church, buying new furniture for Ben's bedroom, and even taking a dance lesson.

I'm just so grateful for that dream. It nudged me step by step to the life I have today. I see Ben more often. We're developing a close relationship. I've paid off my debt. Sarah and I are civil to each other and, though still divorced, work together to be good parents to our son. I've even gotten a better job through one of the guys from my church group. Life is good and it's getting better, one step at a time.

What's Your Next Right Step?

Like Greg, you may feel depressed, uncertain, or just downright stuck in a rut. I'm willing to bet you know more than you give yourself credit for. You know, for example, that at least one or more of the following are true. You want to:

☐   Feel happier

☐   Have more fun

☐   Be healthy

☐   Have more friends and sense of community

☐   Be more confident

☐   Have more money

☐   Be part of the human race again

☐   Find work that you love

☐   Be in a loving, committed partnership

☐   Feel joy again

☐   Have more faith

I'd like to give you a technique I call "the next right step." Every item mentioned on the list above may be on your wish list, but for the sake of this exercise I'd like you to choose the one that most resonates with you right now.

Here are the rules:

- Every day, I'd like you to take one step toward whatever you've chosen. These needn't and shouldn't be huge action steps. They should be baby steps.
- These actions should be things you want to do. You want these steps to be intuitively inspired. This means when you wake up in the morning, ask yourself, "What feels exciting, interesting, compelling today?"
- If you feel drained, bored, or uninterested in any of the steps you've chosen, it's your intuition telling you it's not the right time, it's not the right step, or something else is out of harmony. Don't do it, even if your logical mind is telling you it makes sense.
- If you absolutely need to take an action but don't feel inspired, see if you can break the task down into smaller pieces that do feel interesting.

Here are some examples:

I'd like to have more fun. Today I will:

1. Call Mary. She always makes me laugh.

2. Get the directions for the museum and plan a trip to visit there.

3. Buy a good novel and look forward to curling up and reading it.

I'd like to find work that I love. Today I will:

4. Suggest a coffee with my neighbor. She seems to love her job, and she knows lots of people.

5. Ask Steve about the career coach he worked with after he was laid off.

6. Read the article I found on the Internet about advice for career changers.

I'd like to feel healthier. Today I will:

7. Skip the news and go to bed an hour earlier.

8. Take a walk outside even if it's just to the end of the street and back.

9. Take some slow, deep breaths when I feel stressed.

I'd like to have more friends and a sense of community.
Today I will:

10. Call Joanne and see if she's free for lunch this week.

11. Attend the prayer group that Suzanne has been telling me about.

12. Look into volunteering at the local animal shelter.

You get the idea! These don't have to be big things that will overwhelm and discourage you. At the end of the week, you'll have seven things you've done to make yourself feel better! At the end of the month, you'll have at least thirty. Each day you are making a powerful statement to yourself and the Universe that you are willing to heal, enjoy life, and rejoin the human race.

Again, you may be longing to choose all of the checkboxed items from the list above. Trust me on this . . . if you simply choose one, all the rest of the things you desire will begin to fall into place. You are checking in with your inner compass each day and relying on its wisdom to point you in the direction of . . . more joy, better work, abundance, love, and health. It's a reliable and trustworthy guide. It's been with you since you were born. It's there to help you live the life you were meant to live.

Commit to Action

I believe that taking action is a big key to success for most people. Interestingly, it's also a way to build your intuitive "muscles." I'll explain. Have you ever felt an inner nudge from your intuition to try something new and then completely negated the idea with your next thought? Usually it's something like, "That will never work," or "I don't want to take the risk." You've basically invalidated your inner wisdom. Your intuition will try again and again and again to call out its message to you and get your attention. Each time you fail to pay attention, the intuitive "muscle" shrinks a little and begins to atrophy.

Fortunately, it's fairly easy to rebuild a muscle. Intuition is very forgiving! But it does take commitment to pay attention and to take action on the wisdom you receive. I want to assure you that it is possible to change. It takes (1) the ability to listen, (2) the desire to change, and (3) the ability to take action. It's an unbeatable combination.

Here's another exercise that's based on the next-right-step idea. Get out a pad of paper and on each blank page write something you desire—to get a new job, start a relationship, lose weight, move to another location, get healthier—whatever comes to your heart and mind given your current set of circumstances. List as many positive desires as you want to.

Under each of the desires you've written, write at least ten actions you can take that will help you make a move toward fulfillment of those desires. Again, remember that intuition lets you know, through your sense of excitement or interest, what action to take. Write down action steps that make you feel light and enthusiastic. This shouldn't be just another to-do list.

Joanie had gotten divorced and desperately wanted to move out of the apartment that she and her husband had shared. However, she had been overcome with inertia. I told her about this technique, and here's part of the list she came up with:

Desire: I want to move to a bright, sunny, new, and affordable apartment.

- Action: I'll look online and check out apartment rentals.
- Action: I can stop by that new apartment building on the way home

from work and see if I can look at one of the apartments.

- Action: I'll ask Chris if there are any openings in her building.
- Action: I'll check my lease and see when I can actually leave without a penalty.

After Joanie wrote her list, she felt energized and motivated. She had been trying to push aside the inner voice that had been telling her it was time to move. Making a list of actionable items that were small steps made her feel excited. She had a thrill of anticipation about the new place and a fresh start in life. She called me back a week after the session to tell me she had found a wonderful place and was moving in two months.

You're building your intuitive muscles by continuing to ask, "What do I want?" and "What's the most interesting way to get there?" The answers will come as a flash of insight, a fun idea, a dream, an emotion, an inner whisper, or possibly a bit of synchronicity. These are all ways that your intuition communicates to you. You're learning to live a life where joy is your compass. They probably never taught you that in school!

Be still and listen and then take action.

Do what you can, with what you have, where you are.
—THEODORE ROOSEVELT

YOUR INTUITION JOURNAL

In your journal, write the answer to the following two questions:

1. What do I want to create in my life?

2. What three things could I do today that feel fun, interesting, and/or exciting that will be a step toward what I want?

Remember that intuition will communicate these next steps through a feeling of enthusiasm. If the steps you've written feel boring or uninteresting, choose again!

CHAPTER 13

Powerful Prayer Techniques

The trouble with our praying is, we just do it
as a means of last resort.
—WILL ROGERS

When you're in the middle of a crisis and overwhelmed, it's difficult to find time to pray. Yet when my "Life Transitions" survey asked what was most helpful during tough times, a large number of people answered "prayer." I spoke with, Helen, one of the respondents, about her prayer life.

My sixteen-year-old son, Jake, was in a serious car accident. It was touch and go for many weeks. We really didn't know if he would make it. I was so weighed down during the months that followed his hospitalization. I felt like I was on automatic pilot. I shuttled my other kids back and forth to after-school programs, made meals, tried to work, went to the hospital, dealt with doctors, test results, insurance, and keeping family members and friends apprised of Jake's status. I was barely getting any sleep and relying on caffeine to get me through the day.

    I was raised a Christian, but rarely went to church as an adult, and didn't have a tradition of prayer or even a strong belief in God. It was during a lonely siege of waiting through yet another surgery to relieve pressure on Jake's brain that I got a visit from the hospital chaplain. She simply introduced herself and asked me if she could pray with me. I was so distraught at the moment that I gratefully accepted her offer. She took my hand and offered a simple prayer:

    "Dear Lord, we are thankful for your presence here in this waiting room with us. We feel your healing spirit flowing through Helen, restoring her peace and serenity, giving her strength and fortitude today and through the days that come. Lord, we also

know that you and your angels are with Jake every moment of his day and night. You are restoring him to perfect health. Every cell in his body is radiant with your love and healing. We see him as you see him, in vibrant health and living a normal and happy life. You are the Divine physician who works miracles of healing. We claim Jake's healing in your name. We surrender his care to you. Amen."

As she was saying the prayer, I felt a sense of peace come over me. It was like nothing I had ever felt before. I simply knew that Jake would be well again and that I could handle whatever came along.

Jake took a turn for the better that day. He had a bumpy path on the road to wellness over the next year. But today he is twenty-three years old, with only minor residual effects of his accident. He just finished college and is looking at a bright future. As for me, I now pray daily and consider it an integral part of my life.

The Many Ways to Pray

Like Helen, people often learn to pray when they're in trouble. "Please God, get me out of this situation!" They beseech God to help them find a job, heal their child, restore the love in their marriage, cure them of addiction, or any of the myriad difficulties that may be afflicting them and causing them anguish. There's nothing wrong with pouring out your despair and anxiety in your time of need, and simply asking God for help. However, when you're in the midst of a crisis, it may help to have some techniques or structure.

Sophy Burnham wrote in her wonderful book *The Path of Prayer*, "There is a correct attitude toward prayer, one of humility, of vulnerability, and of surrender. Prayer is the irresistible urge of our human nature to contact and communicate with the source of love, with the energy of the universe. In prayer we ask for help at those moments when we feel totally inadequate to deal with the situation."

It's difficult to think straight when you're overwhelmed, tired, and beleaguered. You may need a simple formula that can bring you to a peaceful place and allow the wisdom and comfort of God to flow to you unobstructed. You come to God as you are. You don't have to be perfect. (Thank God!)

I don't believe there is a "right way" to pray that guarantees access to, and influence by, God. The best way is the one that helps you feel connected to the Divine Presence. Depending on your upbringing, it may help to say a familiar prayer or phrase:

- Our Father who art in heaven . . .
- Baruch Atah Adonai Eloheinu Melech ha'olam—Blessed are You, LORD, our God, King of the universe.
- Assalam u a'laikum wa rahmatu Alla—Peace and mercy of Allah be on you.
- Obviously, the more personal your prayer, the better. Always feel free to change the words to fit your spiritual belief system. Beginning a prayer with "Our Father" or "Lord" may work best for you if you come from a Christian tradition. Saying "I offer my salutations to the Buddhas and bodhisattvas" may be more appealing if you are a Buddhist.

I believe it doesn't matter whether you pray to Spirit, Goddess, Christ, Shiva, Allah, YHWY, or All-That-Is. I most often use the word God because it is familiar to most people. I only know that there is something that is a Creative Intelligent Force that is all around me, within me, and within you. God is part of the sky, the trees, the vast oceans.

While I struggle with the pronoun, I know He exists as immeasurable love and guidance for all. When we pray, we tap into the power of His infinite wisdom to guide us to safety and peace.

Take Time for Quiet

Prayer softens our hearts. It is most often done in moments of silence. Prayer requires vulnerability and openness to make way for something new. It may be a new idea, a belief, or simply a shift in consciousness that allows you to see the world through different eyes.

Simply close your eyes and take a deep breath into your heart. Many spiritual traditions believe the heart is where you connect with the Divine. You are making a request to align with a loving, compassionate force that wants you to be well, happy, and at peace in your life.

Simply watch your breath move slowly in and out. Feel and connect to the Loving Presence in whatever way feels right to you. It might help to bring to mind someone or something you love deeply. This could be your child, spouse, parent, or even your dog or cat.

Imagine being filled with and enveloped by love. Breathe it into every cell of your body. You can bathe in this energy for as long as you like. It is a prayer unto itself. Or you can add some of the other techniques that follow.

Prayer of Protection

One of my favorite prayers is from the Unity Church. It's called "Prayer of Protection." It seems all-encompassing. Whenever I feel upset and need to center myself, these are the words that come to mind:

> *The Light of God surrounds me;*
> *The Love of God enfolds me;*
> *The Power of God protects me;*
> *The Presence of God watches over me;*
> *Wherever I am, God is, and all is well.*

Prayer of Gratitude

The German philosopher Meister Eckhart said, "If the only prayer you say in your whole life is 'thank you,' that would suffice." I understand that it may be difficult to feel grateful when your child is sick, or you just learned of your spouse's infidelity, or the bills are piling up. However, offering an affirmative prayer or gratitude prayer is seeing your situation from the view of perfect healing. You're speaking positive words of faith that your situation is resolved and that you've successfully made it through adversity.

> If the only prayer you say in your whole life is "thank you," that would suffice.

Gratitude prayers might sound like, "I am grateful for the ability to not only pay my bills but also have an overflow of money to help others. I know that you are the source of all true prosperity and I open myself to allow your abundance."

Another example is, "I am open and receptive to your healing presence that flows through me like a river. I am restored to perfect health. Every cell in my body is healed and vibrant with well-being. I'm filled with harmony and peace."

Speak from Your Heart

In a way we are praying all the time. It might be simply, "I'm having a really tough day and I could use some help," or "I'm feeling stuck and need some insight to help me move forward." Just let God know what is on your heart at each moment of the day. As I was writing this chapter, I kept praying, "God, help me to write wise words that will comfort people, let them know you, and allow your wisdom to guide them." Hopefully, my prayer was answered!

A Hindu Prayer

I like this Hindu prayer that seems to cover all bases of our worldly concerns.

In the darkness that encircles us all around, and shuts our vision, do Thou, Lord, rise like the sun, and dispel the darkness with Thy Light Divine. May all be freed from dangers. May all realize what is good. May all be motivated by noble thoughts. May all rejoice everywhere. May all be happy. May all be free from all diseases. May all realize what is good and healthy. May none be subject to misery. O Lord, lead us from the unreal to the Real. Lead us from darkness to Light. Lead us from death to Immortality! Peace, peace, peace be unto all!

An Islamic Prayer

Here's a prayer of healing from the Islamic tradition.

Almighty God! Lord of humankind: remove the hardship and release the sick of her/his sickness. Ease the suffering and heal him/her as you are the Healer. There is no cure except through your healing. Help us to be steadfast and make our faith well established. Grant us a healthy heart and a truthful tongue. Set right our affairs and forgive us our sins, our wrongs, our mistakes, and shortcomings. Amen.

The Twenty-third Psalm

This is probably one of the more popular prayers from the Bible.

The Lord is my shepherd, I shall not want. He makes me lie down in green pastures; He leads me beside still waters; He restores my soul. He leads me in right paths for His name's sake. Even though I walk through the darkest valley, I fear no evil; for you are with me. Your rod and staff support me. You prepare a table before me in the presence of my enemies; you anoint my head with oil; my cup overflows. Surely goodness and mercy shall follow me all the days of my life, and I shall dwell in the house of the Lord forever.

A Common Blessing

I remember this one from the Protestant church I attended as a child.

The Lord bless us and keep us. The Lord keep all those whom we love, whether here or in some other place. May God be our companion and friend, as we walk together through all the days of our lives; and at the journey's end, may we find the welcome of God's love. It keeps us all. Amen.

Buddhist Lovingkindness Meditation

This Buddhist prayer is meant to be said slowly and deliberately, dwelling on the meaning of the words.

May I be filled with lovingkindness. May I be well. May I be peaceful and at ease. May I be happy.

May you be filled with lovingkindness. May you be well. May you be peaceful and at ease. May you be happy.

May we be filled with lovingkindness. May we be well. May we be peaceful and at ease. May we be happy.

You can also fill in an individual name in these blessings. *"May John be filled with lovingkindness. May John be well,"* and so on.

Drive-Time Prayer

When you're in a crisis, it seems like the one commodity you most need is time. If you find yourself spending a lot of time in your car, make it prayer time. As you sit in the driveway or in the parking lot, place your hands on the wheel. Close your eyes, take a deep breath, and ask God to steer you through your day.

My client Karen says she does this every morning before leaving for work. Instead of a to-do list, she thinks of her to-be list. She spends her drive time dwelling on qualities she'd like to develop such as "patient," "calm," and "compassionate." As she thinks of a word, she imagines she is breathing in the quality. Karen feels it has helped her immeasurably as she combines a full-time job with caring for her aging parents.

Walking Prayer

When your mind is overly busy with anxiety, to be still and pray is often an exercise in misery. It's difficult to quiet your overactive thoughts enough to find a center of calm in prayer. There's a Native American saying: Never let a day go by without touching the earth with your foot. So, take a prayer walk. It doesn't need to be a long one. Just ten to fifteen minutes is enough to connect with God's bounty in nature. Breathe deeply. Surrender to this moment that is yours alone with God. Feel free to tell him what's on your mind and ask for guidance or just be present with your surroundings. Use all your senses. Hear the birds, feel the breezes, smell the fragrance in the air. You'll come back from your walk restored and refreshed.

Lunch Prayers

Kelly's six-year-old son, Lucas, was having a tough time in school. He has learning disabilities and they had recently moved, causing him increased anxiety. Each morning when she made Lucas's lunch, she would add prayer thoughts along with his sandwich. She would ask for God's blessing on her child, praying for his inner strength and persistence. Kelly also added a Post-it note to the sandwich bag with affirmations such as "Every day you're getting better and better" and "God is helping you with your arithmetic today."

Lucas loved his notes. Kelly said they were very motivating to him. When he came home from school, she would ask, "What good thing happened to you today?" She felt the question got him more focused on what he liked at school, and his change in attitude began to positively affect his school performance.

What ritual can you create as a way of checking in with God every day? It needn't be formal, complicated, or time consuming. It can be as simple as saying, "Hello, God. It's me. I'm open to your Divine guidance today. I'm going to sit here for a few moments to listen to your wisdom."

Surely suffering is important to our lives, for doesn't it nudge us constantly toward prayer, and hence toward happiness? Toward love? In suffering, our shells are broken open. We are accessible, teachable, guidable.
—SOPHY BURNHAM

YOUR INTUITION JOURNAL

Times of chaos, uncertainty, and transition are facts of life for all of us. Make room for prayer. Even if it's only for five minutes when you wake up in the morning or go to bed at night, make the connection. Prayer aligns you with God's love and wisdom and helps you find calm strength within.

Today as you sit in prayer, keep your journal open. Record any words, images, feelings, or impressions you receive.

CHAPTER 14

The Miracle of Prayer

*The wisest people are those who, although unrelenting in
the quest for answers, trustingly leave some of the problems
in the hands of God, who knows the whole.*
—THE REVEREND DALE E. TURNER

Rosemary had been married for twenty-nine years when her husband announced that he wasn't happy and wanted a divorce. Things promptly went from bad to worse. She discovered that her husband was having an affair with a much younger woman and, to make matters much worse, the woman worked in the same building as Rosemary.

> *I felt so out of control during this time. My work suffered and I couldn't take the stress of running into the "other woman" at the office every day. Also we lived in an old house that needed major upkeep and I felt totally overwhelmed by it. I finally decided to quit my job and sell the house.*
>
> *My family was extremely worried about me. I couldn't eat or sleep during much of this transition. All I knew how to do was to pray. I kept asking for guidance to show me the way. My main prayer during this time was very inelegant: "God, I can't take this anymore, please handle it for me." He did.*
>
> *The changes didn't happen overnight, but I was ultimately led to the perfect home that I absolutely love. I also have a new job with people who appreciate me, and my children have newfound respect for me. I'm even thinking about starting a business to help others who are going through a similar nightmare.*
>
> *I'm still experiencing the effects of the divorce, but I also know that things that look like stumbling blocks are actually stepping-stones. They help to guide you to the arena of your purpose, mission, and successful life you were meant to live.*

I couldn't have gone through this without prayer and listen-
ing to the guidance I received. I know that God continues to work
through me to co-create this new life.

Your Mind and Heart Open to Receive Wisdom

Prayer is a conduit for connecting to a loving, universal force most of us call God. It's about opening your heart, mind, and spirit to receive a higher wisdom and to be influenced and guided by it. A prayer is a request for connection, love, healing, and instruction from a wise and Divine presence. When you tune in to God and allow God to flow through you, your mind and heart become open to inspired ideas and actions.

We often learn to pray authentic prayers when we're in a crisis, when life has turned upside down. There are no atheists in foxholes, as the saying goes. We need help, and our own limited, mortal mind cannot make sense of what's happened to us or help us find the nearest exit to escape our misery. Matthew Anderson, author of *The Prayer Diet*, wrote, "Our prayer does not emerge from our hearts and fly out into the nothingness of space. It is heard without hesitation by a God who cares unconditionally about every aspect of our lives."

When you pray and meditate, you attune your heart, mind, and spirit to God. You become a channel for His wisdom to guide you. You are inviting realignment when you've gotten out of balance or are stuck in fear and anxiety. It's as if God is downloading the code to help set you right again.

Prayer Opens the Path to Miracles

As Rosemary put it, "I had to realize that I was deserving of the best that the Universe had to offer. I prayed often and learned to listen to the guidance that was given. Each day reaffirmed that I need to let go and let God come into my life. He spoke to me through my intuition. When I listened, things worked out and my life turned around."

Prayer opens the channel for miracles into your life. It is an energy transmission that is being sent by God to make you strong in the broken places. He responds to our prayers with understanding, compassion, and love. Even when you don't know what to do, God is lighting the way to the next right steps that will lead you back to peace.

In the silence of reflective listening that follows prayer, simply be still. The silence allows the Divine to work a magical alchemy—calming you, bringing you peace, providing insight and wisdom. Even at the times you feel most abandoned and alone, there is a higher power at work in your life, helping to bring you friends, work, abundance, healing, and love. Rest, relax, and stay open to its wisdom. You are being guided each step along the way.

Prayer is from the heart. It doesn't matter if you use the "right" words or concepts. Tell God what's in your heart. If you're scared and want to feel at peace, say that. If you're out of work and want a job, talk to God about what kind of work you're seeking. If you're going through a painful divorce, let God know how you feel and ask for comfort.

My client, Mary, spoke about receiving an answer to a prayer.

I found that I could let go and trust that a wisdom greater than me, who had my best interests at heart, was guiding me along my journey. God had not forgotten me. I hadn't drifted off my path. God was simply redirecting me and preparing me for something new and greater.

I had to wait, be patient, and let it unfold. When I could sur-render into that idea, things began to happen. A new job showed up that was perfect for me. I wish I hadn't worried so much. That was really what created so much suffering for me. My hope is that I can retain this faith for all future unfoldings.

While I was raised in the Methodist Christian tradition, my family wasn't religious or spiritual. I said my prayers before I went to bed each night. "Now I lay me down to sleep, I pray the Lord my soul to keep; And if I die before I wake, I pray the Lord my soul to take." (That sounds a little scary now that I read it!) I followed this with a long list of "And God bless my sister, my mom, my dad, my dog Jeepers, and all the people who are hungry in the world." (Food was a big thing for me then!) Beyond that I didn't really understand the concept of prayer.

Simply Talk to God

I remember having a conversation with a monk I met in my early twenties. I quite earnestly asked him to teach me how to pray. He looked at me with total bewilderment as if I'd asked him how to breathe. He shrugged and said, "You just talk with Him." I felt mystified and disappointed in his brief answer, wanting something more complicated and, well . . . spiritual. Now I understand that it really is that simple.

Prayer is talking to God. Meditation is how you listen to God. Intuition is one of the ways that answers come. Prayer is based on the premise that you live in a safe universe. God is a God of love and compassion. There is a Wise Presence that guides you, is present with you always, looks out for you, and wants what is best for you like a loving parent. It is God's good pleasure to give you what you need and want, not only to survive, but also to thrive.

When you pray, you may feel inadequate to deal with your current situation. You are humbly resting your concerns on, and surrendering them to, a loving God. You make contact with your in-dwelling God who knows the answers and can provide solutions to set your path right again. We pray to God, but also from God. God resides within us as a thought, idea, hope, love, and new direction.

To change your world you must begin by changing your thoughts. Keep your focus on what you want. When your life turns upside down, you want to be happy again. You want to feel whole, prosperous, healthy, purposeful, and at peace in your world. Pray from the place of the solution. Ask for guidance knowing that the answers are there. Your task is to open your heart, your mind, and your spirit to receive Divine guidance that will redirect you.

Prayers for the Worried

When you're in a crisis, it's all too common to concentrate on what you don't want. Your thoughts are powerful things. Have you ever noticed that if you're worried about something, your attention gets drawn to any and all evidence that this worry is true and real? I spoke with a man named Carl recently. He was concerned that some chest discomfort he was experiencing was a potential heart condition.

I became filled with fear. I called my doctor, but while waiting for the day of my appointment I was drawn to news reports about heart attacks. Everywhere I turned there seemed to be evidence of my worry. I was increasingly agitated. Friends would inexplicably start talking about people they knew who had died of a heart attack. I turned the radio on to hear that a famous person had emergency open-heart surgery. After several days of this, I began to become conscious of the idea that my focus on my fears were like a negative prayer.

I realized I needed to set my mind on a new train of thought. I decided to say things to myself like, "The power of God is within me guiding my thoughts" and "I allow and experience Divine healing in every cell of my body." The affirmative statements were like mini prayers and made me feel calmer.

When I finally got my checkup it turned out that I had a mild heart arrhythmia. It wasn't life threatening. It was treatable. My doctor suggested that it might have been set off by the recent stressful events in my life. It was a wake-up call to shift my focus to the thoughts and actions that made me feel at peace. When I pray from that place, I feel uplifted, safe, and healthy.

Like Carl, you can begin to concentrate your thoughts and pray from the solution rather than the problem or crisis. Ask yourself, "What would my life be like if this situation were resolved?" Hold that picture firmly in your mind as you pray. You'll begin to replace the self-defeating thoughts by holding the vision of your highest future.

Aligning with Your Success

You can start reprogramming your mind today. See your success. Visualize it. Feel it. Sense it. Imagine it. Start believing that you can, and will, shift out of whatever current crisis you're in and move toward a change for the better. The Law of Attraction, metaphysics, spiritual principles, and psychology all agree—you move toward what you see in your mind. When you open your mind to envision the new happy, healthy, and prosperous you, you're aligning with Source that wants these things for you, too. You're also aligning with the information and wisdom that can help you take the best, most direct path to these victories.

No matter what difficulty you're experiencing or how complicated it may seem, prayer can bring about miracles. When you pray, you are claiming Divine Guidance. If you haven't prayed in a while, it doesn't need to be formal. There's no special prayer technique that has been proven to work better than another. If you weren't raised in a particular religious or spiritual tradition and feel you want more structure, read on.

I believe God hears your intentions and knows your heart. The words don't really matter. Whether you're in deep meditation or simply sitting in your car at a busy intersection, God is there and He's listening.

Intelligence, instinct, and intuition all can be instruments of Divine guidance, and we can have confidence if we believe that our wonderful, positive ideas are created in the mind of God.
—THE REVEREND ROBERT SCHULLER

YOUR INTUITION JOURNAL

Choose a brief prayer or statement that makes you feel calm and restores your feeling of centeredness. Write it in your journal or on a piece of paper that you can easily find in your purse or wallet. Practice saying it when you feel stressed.

For example: "Dear God, open my heart and mind to receive your kindness, love, wisdom, and healing."

CHAPTER 15

Letting Life Be Easy

Good morning. This is God. I will be handling all your problems today. I will not need your help so have a good day.
—SIGN IN A DOCTOR'S OFFICE

I have a confession to make . . .

I sometimes get discouraged.

There, I said it! I've broken the Personal Growth Book Writer's Code of Conduct! I've admitted I sometimes get down and depressed about things in my life. However, I don't usually stay in a grumpy, discouraged place for too long. I'd like to share a story about how I shift myself out of feeling bad.

In 2005 I submitted a book proposal to my agent on the topic of using intuition in business. I was really excited about it. Remember that feeling enthusiastic about something is a clue from your intuition that you're heading in the right direction. Companies had been calling me asking for intuition training for their senior executives, and I wanted to write a book that would include all my techniques and philosophy on the subject.

My agent found a publisher for the book. We decided on a title: *Trust Your Gut: How the Power of Intuition Can Grow Your Business*. I was really excited! I had a great team to work with. My editor was terrific. The marketing people had all sorts of creative ideas about how to promote the book. I was told that it was one of the most requested titles for foreign translations. Life was good. I loved how intuition was leading me in the right direction.

I worked hard on the book, diligently writing every day. I interviewed successful, intuitive businesspeople who shared their stories and ideas. I wrote about my techniques, added new ones, and added some of my own stories. I felt like I was in the flow. The book was pleasurable to write, and I was looking forward to the opportunities that publication would bring.

I Receive Exciting News

It was due out in January 2006. My editor e-mailed me in November to say that the book had sold out of its first print run. This meant that the buyers for the bookstores thought *Trust Your Gut* was going to be a hot seller and they wanted it in their stores. This was highly unusual and definitely good news!

I e-mailed my editor about how thrilled I was about this news. This e-mail inexplicably bounced back to me. A couple of days later I called and left him a voice-mail message. I didn't hear back from him. My agent called the next day to inform me that my editor and marketing team had been laid off. A new publishing company had bought the company I had been working with. He said not to worry. (He knows me well!) Fortunately, the new company was excited about helping me publicize my book. They were as delighted as I was that it had sold out its first print run.

To make any book successful in the marketplace, an intricate dance occurs that involves sending advance releases of the book to the media in the hope of generating interest among the buying public. This is combined with an effort by the marketing and public relation teams to supply the media with news angles and pitches that they can use to help them write about and discuss the book.

The Disaster Occurs

In mid-December, just weeks before my book was to be officially released, I received some disturbing news. Because the book had sold out its first print run to the bookstores, there were no copies left to send to the media. Put simply, this was a disaster. If the media didn't receive copies of the book, there would be no reviews. With no reviews, no one would know the book existed. If no one knew the book existed, no one would buy it. The bookstores would ship all the books back to the publisher.

At the beginning of January, instead of celebrating the sale and promotion of my new book I was looking at its demise. At the end of January, I received a note from the newly hired marketing director. She informed me that she would be working only on promoting the books for next season.

Trust Your Gut was now considered an "old" book. The bookstores began shipping back unsold copies of my book to the publisher.

I now had a stash of the books suddenly available to send to the media. I rallied and began to take action. I sent out books, press releases, wrote articles, wrote my blog, and made follow-up calls to everyone I had sent the book to. Many reporters were interested, but again, it was considered "last year's" book and didn't get much traction.

Yes, I was discouraged. Why had my intuition been giving me such a clear go-ahead when the book seemed almost destined to fail? I did what most normal people do in these situations. I cried. I got mad at my publisher, at God, at the world at large, and basically I allowed myself to feel like a total victim.

Trying to Find the Lesson

"There's a lesson in here somewhere" is my motto when bad things happen. In this case I was darned if I could find it. I felt very discouraged. I'd had big expectations that this book would turn around my career. It would allow me to do more speaking, training, and working as a business intuitive, a field that was just beginning to open up.

After a month I finally made the decision to simply accept the situation. I was tired from all the fruitless effort. I was feeling exhausted—which is a definite sign from intuition that I was headed in the wrong direction. I realized I couldn't change the outcome through sheer will, I could only choose to believe that something good was going to come out of this. Any other way of thinking was making me too upset. I surrendered, and instead of feeling victimized, fearful, and wronged, I chose to feel at peace. While this may sound like a simple decision as you read the words, it was not easy in practice. However, I knew that in order to move on and be open to further guidance, I needed to find a way to get to a balanced and calm place again.

Shifting My Attitude

Throughout the day I'd find thoughts coming to my mind such as, "What if my business doesn't turn around?" "What if I don't get the opportunity to write another book?" "Why did this happen to me?" "What if clients stop calling me?" You get the idea.

I decided that even though I didn't know the answer to any of those questions, continuing to ask them in fear and anxiety wasn't helpful. I made several decisions.

1. As noted above, I made the choice to feel calm.

2. I decided to spend more time in meditation and prayer throughout the day.

3. I would listen within for any intuitive guidance I received, knowing there was a larger plan for my life and that I needed to tune in and receive the wisdom.

4. I would continue to affirm, visualize, and envision the life I want to live.

5. I would put my focus on gratitude for all that I have in my life.

6. I would greet each worried or fearful thought with compassion instead of suppressing it or being mad at myself for thinking it.

I'd like to expand on that last point. If you've been a student of the Law of Attraction, you know the theory that what we focus on expands. If I were to continue to feel victimized and angry, I'm sure that I would have attracted some experiences that would have matched that thought vibration.

We're often told to "watch our thoughts" because "thoughts are things and become real." I don't know about you, but I seem to have been born with a worry gene! This goal of always having optimistic and purposeful thoughts is not something I've been able to achieve. Even though I think it humanly unattainable to be peaceful and optimistic all the time, I still berate myself for not being able to do it!

My Inner Voice

When I meditated and listened within, I heard a consistent message. "Lynn, be kind and gentle with yourself. This situation will turn around and turn out better than you can imagine." As part of this inner voice message, I seemed to understand that there was a larger outworking taking place. Perhaps it was a matter of timing. It may have had to do with helping me release some limiting beliefs I had about myself and my work.

Whenever I found myself thinking fearful or anxious thoughts, I would catch myself and refocus my attention. My intuitive side that speaks with a kinder, gentler, more peaceful voice would speak back. If you could hear my thoughts on bad days, you would have to laugh at me! It was difficult breaking those habits of thoughts. It sounded something like this:

Anxious me:	**Intuitive me:**
"Why did this happen? What if I have to get a new career?"	"Lynn, you know things have a way of working out. Be patient."
"What if they don't this time? What if this is different from all the other times?"	"Lynn, remember all those times that things did turn in your favor. God's delays are not his denials."
"Maybe I'm not meant to do this work in businesses. Maybe I should be doing something else. But what?!"	"Be patient. Sometimes you need to let go of knowing why and trust there is a greater vision behind these happenings. The way is being prepared."

As I continued the process, I became calmer. Some days were better than others. Slowly I began to feel better and more hopeful. I also put my focus on what I was grateful for. My individual clients were still calling. I had a nice home. My stepson was graduating from college. My husband and I were getting along well. I was healthy. I had good friends.

Asking for Peace

I also spent time in prayer and meditation each day. I would sit in my favorite chair in my office, close my eyes, and focus on my breathing. I would try to find a centered place within where I felt calm. Some days I was more successful than others. I asked God to help me align with His peace. I prayed and imagined surrendering my anger and upset to the Universe. I affirmed that this situation with my book and career was only temporary. I declared that I was open and receptive to new ways of being of service in the world.

So often in these situations when I'm surrendering, praying, and meditating, nothing seems to happen for a while. What I observed, though, was that I was feeling better. This was a good thing! No big project landed on my desk. The book didn't immediately get discovered and skyrocket to success. I changed. I simply began to feel easier about it all. I was letting life be easy again.

As I'm writing this, it's just over two years post-book-disaster. Obviously, I've gotten a new book contract! The fear of being unable to publish another book did not materialize. Here's the really interesting part . . . My *Trust Your Gut* book was sold to a Japanese publisher. It was published earlier this year. It was one of the top one hundred best sellers on the Japanese Amazon.com for several months running. It's become a huge success.

In August I was invited to visit Japan for two weeks of lectures and seminars. The talk in Tokyo was to more than 2,000 people. At the end of my first lecture, there was an earthquake measuring 5.2 on the Richter scale. I thought it might be God laughing. I suspect He has a wicked sense of humor!

*You want to speak out and sometimes strike out
to make things happen, but don't forget, God works from
the inside out. You must first look within yourself to
eliminate the fear, the anger, the imbalance in your mind
and life. Then, and only then, can you move forward
peacefully and powerfully to make the changes
needed in the world.*
—Iyanla Vanzant

YOUR INTUITION JOURNAL

What's draining your energy right now? The feeling of being drained or bored by something is a nudge from your intuition to move away from that situation.

Ask your intuition, "What is one thing I can do to let my life be easier right now?" Listen for the answer and write about what you come up with.

CHAPTER 16

The Universe Is on Your Side

Life's challenges are not supposed to paralyze you, they're sup-
posed to help you discover who you are.
—BERNICE JOHNSON REAGON

Jackie sat in the front row of her company's national awards dinner. She had won the Top Salesperson award for two years running. She should have been thrilled. Instead all she felt was exhaustion.

> *I barely made it to the stage. My legs felt like they were in setting concrete. My brain felt fuzzy, and I worried that I wasn't going to get through the brief speech I was supposed to deliver. I had been working virtually nonstop to achieve this great accomplishment and all I could think about was wishing I could be home in bed with my eyes closed.*
>
> *I had recently been diagnosed with chronic fatigue syndrome (CFS). I hadn't told anyone except my husband. I didn't want anyone thinking I couldn't do my job or that I was weak in any way. I thought I could tough it out or overcome it through sheer will- power. I was only 38 years old, but I felt like 108.*
>
> *All my life I have been a "take action and get ahead" kind of girl. I was a high achiever as early as elementary school . . . I wanted to be recognized for my accomplishments. It gave me an illusion of control over my life. If other people liked me, I must be okay.*
>
> *At first I thought the CFS was all in my head and that I could tough my way through it . . . I finally had to confess my secret to my senior manager and to my eternal gratitude she was support- ive, encouraging me to get help and take time off . . .*
>
> *I needed to find a new way of thinking about my health and my life in general. I began working with a spiritually oriented*

therapist, Jeannie, who encouraged me to meditate and learn to listen within for answers and direction. This was very hard for me at first. My mind was a constant buzz of anxiety with thoughts about taking action, charging ahead, and winning at all costs.

Jeannie taught me to simply observe those thoughts with no attachment. Notice them and let them go, then focus again on my breath slowly moving in and out, or to simply put my thoughts on a comforting word or phrase. She gave me permission to just try it for a minute at a time at first. When I was comfortable with that, I could do more.

One morning I was so exhausted I decided to meditate before even getting out of bed. As I lay there, I felt what I can only describe as a wave of love pass through me. Then I heard an inner voice say, "The Universe is on your side." I couldn't get that phrase out of my mind all day. Every time I thought about it I felt a new awareness niggling at the edges of my consciousness . . .

I started to entertain the idea that I could live my life in a new way where relaxation, play, connection with others, and spiritual-ity were key components. This may sound very basic to your read-ers, but to me, this was a whole new concept.

I want to hasten to add that this idea and my acceptance of it did not result in an immediate and dramatic change to my health challenges. I'm now about a year and a half past the initial diagnosis. Physically, much has improved, but I still have a long way to go. I've worked hard at allowing myself time to heal. I'm still listening within and heeding the counsel I receive. It's been a crucial piece of the transformation. Here's how this illness has changed me:

• I left my old job, but have found a new passion in coaching women in sales to find life balance.

- *Despite the continued tiredness and the loss of my salary, most days I feel serene, calm, and tranquil. This is such a different "me" than the hard-charging, anxious person I used to be.*

- *I have two new close friends. I never allowed people to support me or know the "real me" before.*

- *My relationship with my husband is stronger. It was very hard for me to let him take care of me and yet this has brought us so much closer.*

- *This illness and my spiritual seeking has brought me a connection to God. I know that I am guided, loved, and protected. God/the Universe is truly on my side.*

I wish that I didn't have to have an illness to teach me all these things. But I also know I needed a major wake-up call in order to genuinely change my life. I have to say that I'm grateful for what this illness has brought me. I no longer live my life with fear. I have an immense sense of love and connection and I know things will continue to get even better as I heal.

Discovering Blessings and Wisdom

The message that Jackie received—"The Universe is on your side"—is an important one. Understanding the significance of it in her life marked a turning point in her healing. You probably picked up this book because you're experiencing a crisis of some sort. Something inexplicable, unjust, or perplexing has happened to you and you're searching for meaning. Psychotherapist Mira Kirshenbaum is author of the seminal book *Everything Happens for a Reason: Finding the True Meaning of the Events in Our Lives*. She wrote, "We can all discover meaning in what has happened to us—seeing such occurrences as gifts, lessons, or opportunities that we might not have been able to get any other way."

Kirshenbaum's twenty-five years of research on this topic indicated ten universal reasons for the tragedies in our lives. Among them are letting go of fear, radically accepting yourself, becoming a good person, finding forgiveness, uncovering a true talent, accepting true love, and discovering your mission. When I think of Jackie's story, I can see elements of all of these.

Finding the Meaning

When you view your life from the perspective of finding meaning, you stop identifying yourself as a victim of life events. You're not simply an unfortunate person who was randomly stricken with illness, or a failure who can't attract a mate. You're in what Kirshenbaum refers to as "Cosmic Kindergarten."

I will admit that this kindergarten can be a strict school. I've often wished that the school lessons came with a little note attached from God that said, "Here's what you're here to learn: _____. You have only to do _____ and experience _____ and you'll pass with an A+."

Let me try to help you fill in the blanks from your own wise source— your intuition. Instead of thinking that the world is out to get you, shift your thinking. What if the Universe is on your side? What if, as the result of this current crisis, things get better? What if this experience is present in your life right now to enable you to receive what you truly want—more love, abundance, clarity of purpose, happiness, peace . . . you fill in the blanks.

Helping You to Be Your Most Authentic Self

What if the world is weighted in your favor? This one shift in thinking could change your life. Most of us approach our lives with our guard up. We're on the alert for something untoward to befall us. We're wary of trouble. Instead of this defensive mode of approaching life, start thinking this new thought: "What if this experience is paving the way for something new and wonderful?" It's the kind of belief that paves the way for miracles.

Try this intuitive exercise to receive guidance about your specific challenge. Take a few deep breaths and center yourself. Say out loud or silently, "I believe that everything happens for a reason. The reason I'm experiencing _____ is to learn _____." Again, you fill in the blanks. The answer may come as a thought, a feeling or emotion, a fleeting impression, a physical sensation, or a symbolic image. You may also receive the answer at a later time when you're not so intensely focused on the response.

I've been working as a professional intuitive for over twenty years. People often come to see me or call me once or twice a year. They usually contact me when they're in the midst of a crisis. The next time I hear from them the emergency has usually transformed itself or ended. It's given me a fascinating perspective on how a challenging life event can heal and help people over time. Let me give you two examples:

David had been a senior analyst in the same corporation for fifteen years. People liked him, he was paid well, and he was in what most would call a plum job. The problem was, he hated it. He said he was worn out and uninspired by his work. He had spoken with me several times about leaving his company, but admitted he couldn't muster the courage to actually do it. One day he called me in a panic telling me that he'd been laid off after a merger. We spent an hour discussing options and possibilities. He left my office feeling hopeful with some action steps to take, including my suggestion to see a career coach.

I ran into David at a social event about a year later. I actually didn't recognize him when I saw him. He had lost weight. He was dressed stylishly. He seemed more confident. He told me that it had taken about seven months to land a new job. But he had used his time off wisely. He saw the career coach and got clear about his purpose and mission. He exercised at the gym, learned to meditate, and got together with friends. He loved his new job—and the best news was that he'd just gotten engaged to a wonderful woman. "I know none of this would have happened if I was still in that old job."

Mary was a high-powered senior executive at a big Boston insurance company. She came to see me shortly after she was diagnosed with breast cancer. She was in the midst of chemotherapy and was exhausted from the rigors of the treatment as well as scared about her future.

I saw her again a year later. She had accepted early retirement at her company and sold her house. She told me it had been a harrowing time and taken a lot of courage. However, she was now decorating a new, smaller place by the ocean. "I feel such peace. I've always wanted to live here, but life seemed much too complicated. Having breast cancer has helped me strip life to its most basic. I'm finding such joy in this simplicity. I've made new friends and I'm happy." She was volunteering at a local hospital helping other women going through this frightening diagnosis.

The Choice Is Yours

Some of us fear our inner guidance because it often leads us to something scary or outside our comfort zone. Viewed a different way, however, it can also lead us to new cycles of learning, growth, and spiritual wisdom. The discomfort or confusion you feel is actually your intuition directing you to make choices in your life that will allow you to break free.

Even when you're in the midst of a huge crisis, you have a choice. You can choose to feel miserable and victimized. Or you can choose to feel guided and directed despite your circumstances. Which do you think would feel better?

Often God shuts a door in our face, and then subsequently opens the door through which we need to go.
—CATHERINE MARSHALL

YOUR INTUITION JOURNAL

Be willing to entertain the possibility that the Universe is on your side. The crisis you're experiencing is helping you to be reborn to something new and wonderful. It's helping you to be strong in the broken places. If you're open to it, the experience can pave the way for miracles. The following questions might be helpful in shifting your thinking:

What are the situations in your life that you feel angry and resentful about?

How could you think about these situations differently that would bring you peace of mind?

What small step or shifts in thinking are you willing to commit to?

Chapter 17

Embracing Fear

We can never know what strengths and revelations might be on the other side of our fears until we face them and feel them all the way through. True positive thinking is the mental stance of surrender, simply trusting the process. We learn to accept what is.
—Jacquelyn Small

Alexis is one of my "Life Transitions" survey respondents. As I read her answers to my online questions, I couldn't believe someone had experienced all these horrible things and was still alive. When I actually spoke to her, she was not only alive, but vibrant, funny, successful, and incredibly positive.

> *I grew up in the worst projects in Boston. I'm the oldest of seven children. I was stealing food to feed my brothers and sisters when I was only fourteen. Life was always difficult. My parents were both alcoholics. They abused my siblings and me both mentally and physically yet I was also their caretaker after they went out on three- or four-day drinking binges.*
>
> *My father lost millions of dollars through his gambling and substance abuse. He was finally sent to prison for robbing a bank with my uncle. They were both heavily intoxicated at the time. I visited him three times a week during the eighteen months he was in jail.*
>
> *When I was sixteen, I took care of my dying grandmother and watched an uncle become consumed and eventually die from drug addiction. When I was twenty, I lost my younger brother when he drowned while attempting to escape from jail. He was only eighteen. They found his body three weeks later.*
>
> *At thirty-five years old I had been married for two years and had a beautiful thirteen-month-old daughter. Unfortunately,*

around this time we found out she had a serious illness. My hus-band couldn't take the stress and bailed out, filing for divorce. He took everything we owned. He even sold the playpen, crib, and our daughter's toys. He also left me $150,000 in debt from the failure of a business he had started.

I decided I couldn't let myself sink into failure. Despite the circumstances I was raised with and the ones I was currently fac-ing, failure was not an option. I became tenacious and resolute. I began to visualize my life as I wanted it to be. I knew that I needed to embrace my fear and embrace life. I couldn't let myself become one of the walking wounded. I wanted to live my life in full vibrant color, not black and white.

I didn't have faith for most of my life. However, when I became pregnant with my daughter, I knew there had to be some-thing much bigger than me to have this miracle happen. I felt an intense desire to explore spirituality. When I was going through my daughter's illness and the divorce, I realized I had to make my faith internal. I had to "paint the picture" of my life, to see it, feel it, breathe it, and work with my Higher Power to co-create it in all ways. When I am in this mind-set, I stay true to who I am and have faith in the outcome.

Today it's sixteen years post-divorce. My daughter has healed and become a lovely, healthy young woman. I've chosen to see my entire life as a blessing. For example, if I had never married, I wouldn't be blessed with my wonderful daughter. I've come to understand that we all have "dark nights of our soul" and at times they seem to go on forever. People often assume I grew up in a lov-ing, harmonious, and affluent environment. I'm well educated and well read and have been very successful in my own business as a consultant in the wellness industry. My intuition has guided me every step along the way. I learned I had the answers within all along. I pay attention to its wisdom and it has served me well.

My advice for others is to know that things will get better. Perhaps not in the way you think they should or on a time frame you've set, but they will get better. Give yourself time to heal. Realize that negative energy, fear, and anxiety are normal, and that you must embrace it all in order to move forward and not stay "stuck." Feel your emotions; cry and laugh and remain open. Pay attention to your own inner wisdom. Your life direction comes from within, not from others. Trust yourself, believe in yourself, and have the mind-set, "Failure is not an option. I can get through this to something better."

Alexis's story illustrates the power of our inner voice in challenging times. Intuition doesn't necessarily steer us away from danger or crisis. However, it's always there whispering wise guidance. It may be giving the message to try something new, offering a different perspective on a program, or encouraging us to take a risk to move in a new life direction.

Let Peace and Harmony Rule

As Alexis noted, fear is a constant companion for most of us when we're going through a difficult time. It seems virtually impossible to stop the what-ifs in our head once they start their drumbeat. "What if I lose my job?" "What if I can't care for my child?" "What if my house goes into foreclosure?" It may be normal to be scared, but taken to an extreme it will leave you paralyzed and unable to act to change your situation.

It's difficult to make positive choices to steer yourself in a new direction if fear is gripping the wheel. I love the guidance about fear that author Sophy Burnham received from her intuition. She shared it in her book *The Path of Prayer.* "Don't fret," said the voice. "You have nothing to worry about! Just relax and let things come along in their proper time. Let Quiet, Peace, and Harmony rule and avoid stressful situations. Let them be born, live and straighten out pleasantly, not with fretting or urgency but by simply accepting the fact—it will work out if you let yourself be led instead of trying to force matters. All is well and remains well." Isn't that incredibly comforting?

Accepting Fear

What do you want to do when something becomes overwhelming and you're afraid? You want to run away! The fight-or-flight mechanism kicks in. If only you had a magic wand to make the situation go away. You wish you could click your heels like Dorothy in *The Wizard of Oz* and voilà, you're back in Kansas (or wherever safety resides). What else can you do when fear has you in its icy grip? You can relax and embrace it.

Fear, or any other emotion, rarely stays static. It changes, moves, goes up and down, in and out. If you can simply accept fear and embrace it, it will begin to lose its power over you. I've found that if I can look deeply into the thing I'm scared about, rather than running away, I can shift its hold on me.

Try this: Ask yourself, "What am I really scared of?" and write down the answer. Ask yourself, "If that thing I'm scared of actually happens, what will I do?" Keep repeating this exercise until you've exhausted your possibilities of fearful outcomes. What I usually find when I do this exercise is that I end up feeling mildly amused by all the unlikely scenarios my mind can come up with.

Former first lady Eleanor Roosevelt wrote, "You gain strength, courage and confidence by every experience in which you really stop to look fear in the face. You are able to say to yourself, 'I lived through this horror. I can take the next thing that comes along.'" Fear is not something you fight. It's something you make room for in your life. Embrace it and make it your ally, not your enemy.

> 'I lived through this horror. I can take the next thing that comes along.'

Take Action

Fear can permeate our minds if we allow its negativity in there for too long. Fear is the sister of worry . . . It takes on a life of its own, convincing us of our own worthlessness and ineffectiveness. Popular speaker and minister Joyce Meyer wrote, "God doesn't want us to be scared. But even when we do feel fear, we can choose to trust God and take action."

I've found that the best antidote to fear is action. If you have become immobilized by fear, start asking yourself, "What one thing could I do today that would make me feel better?" It can be something simple and easy or something major and audacious. When asked a question like this, your intuition will begin to offer suggestions. It might be to have coffee with a friend, writing a note to someone you need to forgive, being brave enough to make an appointment with a financial planner, or seeing a therapist or other healing professional.

Philosopher Ralph Waldo Emerson wrote, "Always do what you're afraid to do." And former first lady Eleanor Roosevelt advised that we "do one thing every day that scares us." Trust that whatever sparks your interest or curiosity is the right answer. It may not make sense, but do it anyway! That's the way intuition works. You know something or feel nudged to do something, but you often have no idea why!

On the other side of every fear is freedom. You'll find the freedom, in part, by taking action. It begins to get you unstuck from your old thinking, your old way of being and behaving that partially contributed to your current life circumstances. Instead of fighting with the fear, have it join you on your action journey.

The Small-Step Action Plan

Robert Maurer is the author of *One Small Step Can Change Your Life*. I think it should be required reading for anyone who is experiencing a crisis or simply feeling stuck. His technique is undeniably simple. It also taps into your own inner wisdom to provide the answers you seek and helps you overcome fear and inertia. His philosophy is that small steps are things that all of us can do. They add up to big changes because they're doable and manageable. Obviously, his book provides much more detail, but here's a brief overview:

1. Ask small questions. "If health were my first priority, what could I be doing differently today?"

2. Think small thoughts. Think of a task or situation that makes you uncomfortable or fearful. Spend a few seconds (not minutes) each day on visualizing a successful outcome.

3. Take small actions. Examples: If your goal is to stop overspending, a small action might be to remove one item from your shopping cart before heading to the register. If your goal is to manage your stress better, a small action could be to take one deep breath.

4. Solve small problems. You'll often receive intuitive messages about an impending crisis well before the crisis arrives. For example, you'll slow down while driving if you sense a dangerous traffic situation up ahead. Don't ignore early warning signs. Listen. Pay attention and act on the information you're receiving.

Ask for Help

While I was writing this chapter, my doctor informed me that a relatively small health challenge was going to require surgery to head off future problems. I'm someone who would prefer not to take as much as an aspirin, and the thought of surgery, however minor, sent my mind into a fear tailspin. I immediately did some Internet research, which only increased my anxiety.

After a day of envisioning all sorts of nightmare scenarios, I finally decided to practice what I preach. I sat down, took a few slow deep breaths to center myself. I asked my intuition, "What can I do to feel calm and peaceful right now?" My inner voice delivered up a three-word answer: "Ask for help." That may sound very simplistic. However, I'm usually the one who helps other people. My normal coping method in a crisis is an overly independent, "I can handle things myself."

I did what my intuition suggested and began calling friends to let them know what was going on. After a few conversations I felt surrounded by love and caring and the simple realization that people want to help and appreciate being sought out. Suzanne offered her visualization techniques. Barbara offered to bring over a meal or two. Gail offered practical information from her background in the medical field. My anxiety transformed to a calm acceptance and gratitude and I felt okay with the idea of the surgery.

Try this: If you notice panic rising, reach out to someone. Call a friend. Send an e-mail. You're just communicating, "I'm having a tough day. Talking to you makes me feel better." If you're isolated and lacking friends, say a simple prayer: "I am open to welcoming others into my life." The important thing is to counter the kind of "fear energy" that spirals out of control. You want to feel connected to others as well to the Divine spirit that guides you to peace when you feel scared.

Our job as a teacher of God, should we choose to accept it, is to constantly seek a greater capacity for love and forgiveness within ourselves. We do this through "a selective remembering," a conscious decision to remember only loving thoughts and let go of any fearful ones.
—MARIANNE WILLIAMSON

YOUR INTUITION JOURNAL

Imagine that it's five years from now. You have safely moved through this difficult time in your life and on to something new and wonderful.

Write the answers to the following questions in your journal:

- What was the most important thing that helped you get through the times you were afraid?

- What do you know now that you wish you knew then?

- What do you wish you had done differently?

- Given how things turned out, what are you most proud of?

CHAPTER 18

You're on God's Payroll

Billfold Blessing: Bless this billfold, Lord, I pray. Replenish it from day to day. May the bills flow in and out, blessing people all about. Help me earn and wisely spend. Show me what to buy and lend. Thank you, God, for bills to pay, for the things I need today. When 'tis empty, fill it more, from thy vast abundant store. Amen.

—ANONYMOUS

Financial concerns are on top of the list of things that people are worried about when they experience a crisis. An unexpected life event can upend even the most prosperous people. In my "Life Transitions" survey, I've heard from a person whose business partner had embezzled a significant portion of company funds; from working parents who had to leave a job to care for a seriously ill child; and from a man who had lost his life savings in a venture that went belly-up. There were so many stories like these. Here's one with a truly inspirational twist.

Mary prided herself on her frugality. She joked that she felt she had married well because her husband, Mark, shared a similar parsimonious philosophy. They had been in their jobs for fifteen and twelve years, respectively. Mary kept the family on a tight budget and was proud of the fact that at thirty-five years old they had saved a nest egg of $48,000. Their lives revolved around raising their two children, working, going to church, and spending time with friends. Then Mary got sick.

> *I was in the doctor's office for my yearly physical. I felt fine. We were chatting away about our kids, the school system, and whatever and then she just got quiet as she did the breast exam. She felt a small lump. "It's probably nothing. A lot of times these are false alarms. Let's just get it checked with a mammogram."*
>
> *I had gone through this two years before when another doctor*

had found a similar suspicious lump. The mammogram hadn't shown any evidence of a problem. However, I made the appointment she had suggested and a follow-up with her for a week later. I just figured I'd get the same news as last time. But when I saw my doctor's face, I knew the answer wasn't good. It turned out I had stage 2 breast cancer.

Over the next several weeks, life became a blur of sleepless nights, lab tests, doctor appointments, biopsies, and heartbreaking conversations with both Mark and the kids. We had no idea we were going to get hit with yet another crisis so soon after the first one . . . my health insurance company denied coverage for my cancer treatment.

The stress of the cancer diagnosis was awful enough, but the thought of going through all of our life savings and more was hell. Bills were coming in with amounts like $1,300, $3,200, $5,000 and I hadn't even had the surgery yet, no less the radiation and chemotherapy. It was like we were playing with Monopoly money.

During this time I had several conversations with my minister. I was experiencing a great deal of anxiety and was beginning to slip into a clinical depression. One evening he prayed with me and then suggested we just sit in silence and invite God's wisdom. I've always prayed for others—my family, friends, people at work and church—it just never occurred to me to ask for God's guidance for myself.

As we prayed and then sat in silence, I felt an incredible peace come over me. It was like someone had placed a warm shawl over my shoulders. Then I heard a soft female voice say, "Don't worry. You're on God's payroll. You will be well and all will be well." It was so real I actually opened my eyes to see if there was anyone else in the room!

At the end of our silence, I decided to share what I had experienced with my pastor even though I felt a little embarrassed. To my relief, he wasn't the least bit surprised. He said answers to prayers often come in an inner voice. I felt comforted by this thought but also joked that if I was on God's payroll, I was in *need of a big raise! Every day I sat down to pray. I asked God for increased health, faith, and to be open to receiving abundance on His "payroll." I was determined to keep my focus on my blessings—my faith, Mark, kids, community, home, and our small amount of investments.*

Over the next few months, the blessings began to increase. Members of my church heard about our situation and put on a big fund-raiser. My physician waived her fees. A car dealer donated a year-old car to us. Mark's company allowed him to take paid time off to care for me and the kids when I was too sick to do it.

It's now two years post-diagnosis. My doctors tell me I'm cancer-free and I'm choosing to believe them. We just found out that the insurance company will reimburse us for a part of the expenses we've incurred. I'm still here. It has helped us to become closer as a family and community.

Matthew 6:26 reads, "Look at the birds of the air, that they do not sow, nor reap nor gather into barns, and yet your heavenly Father feeds them. Are you not worth much more than they?" I think that's the way the Bible lets you know about "God's payroll." I'm simply glad I listened to that inner voice.

Mary's story illustrated for me the idea of Divine prosperity. We may not know where the money, help, or solution to our situation will come from. The important components are faith, listening to our inner guidance, holding the thought and vision of the outcome we want, and a willingness to receive it.

Make Room for Abundance

What is prosperity? In his book *Spiritual Economics,* Eric Butterworth explained that the word prosperity "comes from the Latin root which literally translates as 'according to hope' or 'to go forward hopefully.'" Thus it is not so much a condition in life as it is an attitude toward life. Prosperity is not a specific dollar amount. It encompasses many things.

A colleague of mine recently defined prosperity by saying, "I know that I have within me and around me a Divine flow of abundance. Whatever my goal, desire, or dream, I have the means and ability to create this thing or situation in my life." What he describes sounds similar to Mary's feeling of being on "God's payroll."

Knowing how to create a prosperous life doesn't imply that everything you wish for is instantly manifested. Mary's medical bills were not instantly paid by a big lottery win, for example. There is a duality of existence that is a bit tricky to master. First, you feel thankful for all that you have. You see abundance around you and focus on it with an attitude of gratitude. And second, you also understand that you are constantly growing, learning, and mastering your world. It's natural for you to want more, to have fresh goals, and to move in new directions.

I'm not suggesting you should jump for joy when you're in the midst of a crisis. However, when your mind is full of anxiety and fear, there's little room for a solution to enter. How do you begin to create that space? You can start by finding a way to shift your thinking and look at your life with gratitude.

Mary told me that she got very sick from the chemotherapy and radiation treatment. It gave her a lot of time to dwell on her fear. She described wrestling her mind off her anxieties and on to what she was grateful for. "Yes, I was very ill. I was also anxious for my family and for our finances and way of life. I could have simply dwelled on that. But I chose little by little to focus on all that we had." She described the love of her husband, the sound of the kids coming home from school, the pleasure she felt at making it to the grocery store to shop after a week of not being able to get out of bed.

Your Inner Prosperity Guide

What if you did, in fact, have an inner prosperity guide who was constantly pointing you toward ever more abundance? What if God really is in charge and wants you to feel safe, cared for, and successful? Mary tapped into this source when she listened to the wisdom she received in prayer.

I love this quote from Henry Ford, the founder of the Ford Motor Company: "I believe God is managing affairs and that He doesn't need any advice from me. With God in charge, I believe that everything will work out for the best in the end. So what is there to worry about?" Ford was one of the wealthiest men of his time. In 1936 he began what has become a worldwide, multibillion-dollar philanthropic foundation to advance human welfare. If it worked for him, it can work for you!

How can you begin to tap into this power? Here is a simple exercise to get you started. As with any of the exercises in this book, feel free to change the words and concepts to fit your own spiritual belief system.

Close your eyes and center yourself with a few deep breaths. As you breathe slowly, begin to use all your senses.

What are the sounds you hear?

The scents you smell?

What do you view around you in your interior landscape?

Observe the rhythm of life flowing in you, through you and all around you.

Be in the present moment and find the place in your heart and soul where you know you are okay.

Continue to focus on your breathing and connect with God in your thoughts. Know you are safe, loved, and protected, and that all the Universe has is yours.

When you feel you have reached this point of connection, say to yourself,

I know that with God all things are possible. My every need is met. I welcome abundance in all forms. I invite Divine "right action" into my life and know that everything is working out for the best for the highest good of all concerned. I accept all the good that God has to offer. I know that my specific situation is being healed. I accept this healing. Amen.

Now ask God, "Is there anything I could do right now to allow this prosperity to flow into my life?" Await a response. And then, when you feel ready, open your eyes.

When I teach this technique in my intuition classes, I often hear a disappointed, "I didn't get an answer!" My response is to finish that statement with the word "yet." You may not have received an answer yet. I believe it's important to know that if you have opened a channel of communication with God, your prayers will be answered.

Receiving the Answer

The answer may not necessarily come in the form of an inner voice like Mary experienced. It's important to have trust and faith in the process. Look for evidence that it is coming your way. The Universe will bring together the circumstances and synchronicities that will enable you to have the prosperity you deserve.

As a way to continue this experiment, you might focus on financial gratitude. When you find yourself starting to feel anxious about money, or you catch yourself complaining about your lack of financial abundance, stop.

Now shift your attention to all that you already have. This might be good friends, your health, terrific kids, an interesting job, and/or wonderful neighbors. Find anything to think about that makes you feel good. Gently shift your attention away from your fear. If you're very impoverished and have been focusing on your lack for quite some time, this may be a tough assignment. But it's a good place to start.

Here are two recent items from my financial gratitude journal:

- I feel blessed that my neighbor has a beautiful swimming pool I can use to enjoy a quiet half hour of relaxation after a day of writing. I don't have to own the pool or put money into the upkeep, but I reap many of the benefits.
- I enjoyed getting together with my friend Gail, who graciously paid for lunch. I value her friendship.

Whenever you find yourself experiencing fearful thoughts about your financial situation, bring yourself back to the present moment. Keep your mind focused on the many things you do have that you can feel grateful about. Everything else you need will follow from there. Gratitude activates your connection to God and His Divine abundance.

We come equipped with everything we need to experience a powerful life full of joy, incredible passion, and profound peace. The difficult part is giving ourselves permission to live it.
—Deborah Rosado Shaw

YOUR INTUITION JOURNAL

Focus on abundance. There is plenty to go around. The Universe has an infinite supply. Welcome and notice the many ways you can receive it.

Begin a financial gratitude section in your journal. Each day write about the financial blessings you've received, large and small. Remember that what you focus on expands!

CHAPTER 19

The Healing Power of Writing

We are cups, constantly and quietly being filled. The trick is,
knowing how to tip ourselves over and let the beautiful stuff out.
—RAY BRADBURY

Leah's difficulties began four years ago when her son was only five months old and her daughter was eight. She learned that her husband, Jerry, was having an affair. It had begun when she was pregnant. Jerry didn't want a divorce, but it turns out he didn't want to end the affair, either. Leah felt she had no choice but to ask him to leave and begin divorce proceedings.

The next few years were incredibly hard. I was caring for a toddler, managing the anxiety of my daughter over the divorce, holding down a full-time job, and dealing with my own grief and remorse. Every day my mind was filled with replaying the scenes from my marriage, my bitterness toward my ex-husband, and self-recrimination over the many things I felt I should have done differently.

Jerry married the woman he was having the affair with. He apparently asked her to marry him before our divorce was even final. I thought I was at the lowest place in my life when suddenly, things got worse. I fell down the front stairs at my house, breaking my elbow, ankle, and knee.

My babysitter had to call Jerry and ask him to pick up the kids. I was in the hospital for five days. It slowly dawned on me that I was so broken and in so much physical pain that I was going to need long-term rehabilitation. I would not be able to care for my children. It was the hardest decision I ever made, but I chose to give Jerry custody of the kids.

I also knew that in addition to healing myself physically, the accident was a huge wake-up call to heal myself emotionally and spiritually. I began seeing a social worker who recommended I write daily in a journal to gain insight and direction. Little by little I moved from self-hatred, victimization, and despair to taking responsibility, feeling self-empowered and capable.

Through the writing, I've also reconnected with God and my Jewish faith. I've learned that my story can be an inspiration to others. I was recently asked to give a talk to my synagogue about what I've learned. People told me they were incredibly moved by my words and outlook on life. This has encouraged me to write and speak about my experiences to help others.

I still struggle with the fact that I'm permanently disabled and in daily pain. It's still hard for me to see the kids only on the weekends. But I've already become more stable physically than my doctors had predicted. Emotionally and spiritually I'm stronger. My journal writing combined with my determination to be happy was a big piece of the healing.

Leah discovered her intuitive voice through her writing. She told me that as she put her pen to paper, the words seemed to pop into her mind. She learned that the words to trust were the ones that were loving, encouraging, and gave her confidence. Those, she knew, were the words from God.

Writing as a Tool for Self-Discovery

Many people write journals for personal reasons such as keeping a diary of daily happenings, gratitude lists, drafting letters they don't send, as well as writing memoirs. Others, like Leah, may work their way through a personal crisis by gaining insight and direction through their writing. In fact, a recent study found that people who wrote fifteen minutes a day about their personal traumas experienced improvement in their physical health and emotional health.

A journal is also a meditative tool for self-discovery, a mirror for the soul, a place to understand yourself and your world, a safety release valve for complex emotions, and a source through which intuitive wisdom may come. Norbert Platt, the CEO of the company that makes the lovely Montblanc pens, wrote, "The act of putting pen to paper encourages pause for

The act of putting pen to paper encourages pause for thought.

thought. This in turn makes us think more deeply about life, which helps us regain our equilibrium."

Some people thrive on journal writing and can claim years of diaries stacked up in the attic or basement since childhood. Others have tried, only to find their interest flagging after a few entries. It may feel overwhelming to commit to a journal, but why not start small? Instead of telling yourself, "I'll write in it every day," try a smaller step like keeping the journal on your desk or bedside table along with a pretty pen, or agreeing to write just fifteen minutes a week at first. If you like it and it's helpful, you'll want to continue. If not, no harm in trying. It may not be for you.

I've personally found it beneficial to have some ideas or themes to write about. These can stimulate intuitive insights. They've especially helped me during times of crisis and general life conundrums. I find I can manage a weekly journal much better than a daily one. I usually write mine on Sunday evenings.

You might find that the following list of questions I use can assist you in getting started. I've had students use these questions to help them do everything from losing weight to attracting a new partner, making more money, establishing a business, or overcoming an anxiety disorder. It's a funny thing—when you ask a question, your mind wants to come up with an answer.

I have a ritual of lighting a candle, playing some calming music, and meditating for a few minutes before I take pen in hand to write.

7 Questions to Ask in Your Intuition Journal

Some people find it helpful to answer these questions once a week at the same time, say a Sunday evening. Others take one question a day and write their response. Do whatever feels comfortable for you.

1. What did I learn this past week?

2. What was I most proud of this week?

3. What was the most fun thing I did this week?

4. What could I do to be happier in the coming week?

5. What could I do next week that will help me reach my goal of ____?

6. I'm struggling with ____. What can I do to make this easier?

7. If my intuition wanted to give me one piece of advice, what would it be?

Please feel free to mix and match these questions and make up ones of your own. The blanks are places to fill in with an issue or dilemma that's specific to you. For example, Leah wrote the following for question 6:

I'm struggling with depression. What could I do to become happy?

Her intuitive answer:

You can't change the past. Let it stay in the past and release it as part of your history. All those events are part of who you are today. Happiness is a choice. Choose to put your focus on what makes you happy right now.

Leah said that she tries to write whatever pops into her mind first without censoring anything. She feels that when the words are loving or make her feel more at peace, it's her intuition speaking. I think she's on the right track. Intuitive answers are not the ones that scold or reprimand you or make you feel worse. Accurate intuition always gives guidance that is clear, kind, and direct.

Intuitive Writing Prompts

If the idea of starting with a question, subject, or issue is appealing, you might try one of the following:

Find a favorite quote.

There are plenty of inspiring quotes in this book. Copy one you like into your journal and then write about why it's compelling to you. The reason you found the quote interesting was perhaps that your intuition was nudging you toward it. Here's a good quote that's designed to inspire. It's from Nelson Mandela in his inauguration speech. "Your playing small does not serve the world. Who are you not to be great?" How could you use messages like this to help you through your current crisis?

Ask the right question.

I recently came across a Dennis the Menace cartoon. In it, Dennis is saying, "I am giving you the right answers! You're just asking the wrong questions!" If you're writing questions of your own for your intuition journal, make sure they're phrased positively. "Why am I so blocked?" and "Why can't I get better?" are examples of Dennis's "wrong questions." Try instead, "What can I do to be more open to life?" or "What could I do to help heal my body?" You see? You're putting the focus on what you want, not on what you don't want.

What are my strengths?

When you're going through a difficult time, it's all too easy to feel weak and helpless. What are you good at? When people pay you a compliment, what do they say? What inner gifts have you called on to get you through past crises as well as this current crisis?

What am I learning?

God often puts detours into our lives to help us grow strong and gain mastery in an area of weakness. It helps to see the reason that may be behind our life challenge. When I've written about this for myself, I'm no longer surprised by the word that usually tops the list: patience. I guess I'm still working on that one. I just wish I would hurry up and get it already!

If I won the lottery, I would . . .

Have you let a lack of money stand in the way of creating a life you love? If so, you may have buried your true passion and mission. Completing this sentence in your intuition journal may help you start to dream about the life you want. When you give yourself permission to dream it, your intuition can begin to direct you toward how to achieve it (with or without the lottery money). I see people minimize their dreams all the time. Ask your intuition to help you dream big.

Just write!

Pick up your journal and pen and write for fifteen minutes. Ask yourself, "What does my intuition want me to know?" Don't censor or edit yourself as you write. If you get a few moments of writer's block, jot that down, too. It will feel like stream-of-conscious brainstorming.

What am I afraid of?

We all feel fearful and anxious at least some of the time. It's human. It's normal. Trying to fight it or deny it doesn't make it go away. Acknowledging your fear and having compassion toward yourself is the best antidote. Draw a vertical line down the center of a page in your journal. On one side, write a list of your ten worst fears. After you've completed this, take a deep breath, put your hand over your heart, and draw in as much love and compassion for yourself as you can muster. Now ask your inner voice, "What could I do to calm my fears?" Go through each fear and write an intuitive response.

When things begin falling apart in your life, there is a Wisdom guiding you that wants to help things come together again. The desire of this Wisdom is that you learn to love, forgive, have compassion, accept love from others, have self-esteem, and share your distinctive gift with the world. One of the ways you can access this inner wisdom is by listening within, writing, and taking steps to claim your unique purpose and mission. Start writing!

*How often in the past have you turned away from
all that is unresolved in your heart because you feared
the questioning? But what if you know that a year
from today you could be living the most creative, joyous,
and fulfilling life you could imagine? What would it be?
What changes would you make? How and where would you
begin? Do you see why the questions are so important?*

—SARAH BAN BREATHNACH

YOUR INTUITION JOURNAL

Begin to collect photographs from magazines, advertisements, brochures, or the Internet that represent something you want to create in your life.

Paste the images in your journal or on a large sheet of poster board. You can put the pictures all on the same page or you might choose to have categories such as "home," "career," "relationship," "health," "finances," or other subject of your choosing.

Look daily at this representation of your ideal life. Ask your intuition, "What steps could I take today toward this wonderful new life?" Act on the information you receive.

CHAPTER 20

The Secrets to Successful Decision Making

Never bring the problem-solving stage into the decision-making stage. Otherwise, you surrender yourself to the problem rather than the solution.
—ROBERT SCHULLER

Most of us hate making big decisions. When you're in the midst of a crisis, life seems to be one big decision after the other. Should I leave this job? Would my life be better if I moved to another place? Is it time to end this relationship? Should I start my own business? How can I make more money? We usually angst about these issues for weeks, months, and even years.

You want peace. You want success and prosperity. You want health. You want love, connection, and community. Which of the myriad decisions in front of you will guarantee all of the above and more? Which path will lead in the right direction? When you include intuition as part of your decision-making process, you're more likely to make a good choice. Your intuition is your inner compass. It will always point you in the right direction.

I've observed that, left to their own devices, most people decide not to decide. They let "fate" take its course. What this actually means is, they don't make an active choice about what they want so much as they let circumstances choose for them. You can't avoid decisions. In fact, to not make a decision is, in itself, a decision. George Bernard Shaw said, "Progress is impossible without change, and those who cannot change their minds, cannot change anything."

> ... those who cannot change their minds, cannot change anything.

Which Decision Feels Best?

People usually call me when they have a decision to make. I don't make the decision for them, but I help them by asking some key questions that allow them to make a good one. I also assist them by introducing them to their intuition. Most people think they need to be 100 percent certain about a decision before they make a move. I have developed something I call the 60/40 Rule about decisions. This is the way it works: If you feel slightly more certain than uncertain that the decision you're about to make is a good one, go for it.

My client Maryann was in severe pain from arthritis in her left hip. She'd consulted her doctor about the possibility of hip replacement surgery. She'd also received second and third opinions from two other doctors. In Maryann's case it wasn't so much if she should have the surgery as when. She was in her early fifties and because the implants often last only ten to fifteen years, there was some value in waiting. Unfortunately, it was the when part of the decision that was causing Maryann a lot of anxiety.

She believed there was only one right decision that would guarantee a successful outcome for her health. Her doctors had all given her varying advice, and so the decision was hers to make based on the information she had gathered. She still felt paralyzed with indecision. There's usually no one perfect answer to any question, and there wasn't one in Maryann's case.

We discussed the fact that Maryann had four main choices in front of her: (1) have the surgery now, (2) wait a few more months or years, (3) find alternative healing methods that might help ease the pain now and in the near future, or (4) seek out more opinions from specialists. Looking at her options in that way eased her apprehension a bit. Narrowing the choices down a bit felt easier.

I asked her to close her eyes, take a deep breath, and find a place of centeredness within herself. She nodded to let me know she'd arrived at that place. I repeated the four choices and then had her ask herself the question, "Which choice feels best right now?" When she had the answer, she was to let me know and continue to stay in that centered place with her eyes closed.

We waited for a moment and then she said, "It feels best to find some alternative healing methods."

I suggested she take another deep centering breath and then ask within, "What are some things I could do to help my hip feel better?"

She immediately came up with four ideas. Take a gentle stretching class. Get a massage once a week. Explore the possibility of acupuncture. Get some emotional support from a friend who was also considering joint replacement surgery.

Based on the 60/40 Rule, this decision felt slightly better than the other choices available to her. When she opened her eyes, she felt much calmer. Her intuition had delivered the answer she needed for right now.

The What-If Response

The other big reason people have a hard time making decisions is that they literally scare themselves by coming up with worst-case scenarios. "What if this happens?" "What if that happens?"

Take the case of Peter. He had been unhappy in his job for almost five years. He had come for several sessions with me during this period, and each time he made a very persuasive case for leaving his job. Among them was the fact that it was a family-owned business. He wasn't a member of the family, and it was obviously limiting his job potential. He was an online salesperson. He was also in an industry that he didn't feel a whole lot of passion about.

His list of dislikes about his current position was long. Yet when I spoke with him about finding a new job, he got stuck in the dreaded what-ifs. "What if I can't find another company I like?" "What if I need to go back to college?" "What if I get another job and I don't like that one, either?" Peter was creating some powerful images of failure in his mind. Every what-if was a mental picture of something not working out. Hence he felt stuck and unable to make a decision.

I suggested that Peter close his eyes and ask himself a simple question: "What would my day look like if I enjoyed going to work?" After a few moments he began to smile. He told me he'd love a job that had a short commute, an informal work environment, and a career that provided him with an opportunity to use his Internet sales and social networking skills.

I gave Peter a two-part assignment:

1. Every day he was to ask himself the question, "What would my day look like if I enjoyed going to work?" He was to jot down any and all ideas that came to mind.

2. I asked him to commit to spending just thirty seconds a day visualizing his ideal job.

Why would this work for Peter and for you? It allows you to engage your mind in a positive way. When you ask some variation of the question, "What would be the best outcome," you're becoming focused on what you want. You're telling your subconscious mind, "This is what success looks like." When you close your eyes and ask the question, your inner wisdom delivers an answer in the form of positive feelings, images, and even words to point you in the direction of the success you desire.

Writing the answers in a notebook or on your computer is helpful. It seems to stimulate intuition. Visualizing an outcome you desire helps your intuition know what you're looking for. It can then come up with ideas and responses that help you manifest it. Finally Peter was able to shift a large decision ("Should I leave my job?") into some small information-gathering steps that were a lot less threatening.

I realize that leaving a steady job in the midst of an economic downturn is not one most of us would make. However, if your intuition is steadily nudging you toward a change, pay attention. You can do as Peter did and begin to honor your intuition by exploring options and asking the questions above to gain clarity and insight into a potential new direction. That way you'll be ready when the time is right.

Turn Big Actions into Little Steps

Peter ended up finding a great job while searching online. One of the things that really helped him, he told me, was that the question we focused on enabled him to take small steps. "I changed my task from 'should I leave my job?' to discovering 'what's fun and interesting to me?' That small shift enabled me to find a job without a lot of effort. I wish I'd done it years ago!"

Holly had a similar experience. She had recently been laid off from a corporate job due to downsizing. She had always toyed with the idea of starting her own graphic design business. She figured this was the perfect time to make the decision. Instead she found herself paralyzed with doubt and didn't know where to begin. "I know what I want. I just can't figure out how to get there."

Holly was at the beginning of the path to a new career and needed some decision-making tools to help her create a successful business. She was overwhelmed with how to get from "here" to "there"—a full-fledged, rewarding, graphic design business that could bring her a decent income.

I came up with the "next step" method of building my business. I realized there wasn't a one-size-fits-all model for success. I had to take my skills, abilities, aptitudes, and interests into account to create a business that would work for me. I meditated every morning shortly after I woke up. As I finished my meditation, I would ask myself one of a series of questions that would help me determine my successful action for the day. Here are my top seven favorite questions that got me motivated:

1. What can I do today that will help me grow my business?

2. What's one step I can take that will help me reach my goal today?

3. Whom could I ask for help today?

4. What's special about my talent and service and how could I communicate that to a potential customer today?

5. Who do I know who is successful in their business and how could I emulate them today?

6. What fun, creative way could I promote my business today?

7. What person or business could I approach today to tell them about my services?

> *When I meditated on the question, I'd find an answer would pop into my mind. Obviously, I'm very visually oriented because my business is graphic design. I'd find the answers would come mostly in images, too. For example, to question 1, an image of a funny cartoon came to mind. I used that in a successful direct-mail postcard campaign.*
>
> *Sometimes the answers are a little weird, but I've come to trust them. To question 6, I received an image of walking my dog in a nearby park. That seemed to have nothing to do with promoting my business, but I figured I got the answer for a reason. Lo and behold, I met another dog owner in the park who had also just started a business, and he needed help with a logo and a design for his Web site!*
>
> *This method of taking small steps has all but eliminated the feeling of being overwhelmed I'd experienced initially. It's become a fabulous way to market my business. I call it my intuitive business plan!*

Kind Questions Evoke Intuitive Answers

One of the other main reasons people get mired in making decisions is they beat themselves up! "Why am I such a jerk?" "Why can't I stick to this diet?" "Why do other people get all the breaks?" "Why am I so stupid?" As I mentioned earlier, framing questions positively is helpful in eliciting positive answers.

The questions that Holly asked were all constructive ones that were effective at stimulating her intuition. She didn't ask, "Why can't I figure out how to create a successful business?" She asked kind, creative questions and her intuition responded similarly.

How do you know when you've received an intuitive answer? It makes you feel good. It is kind, positive, creative. It feels uplifting. Neale Donald Walsch, author of the "Conversations with God" series of books, wrote, "Life begins at the end of your comfort zone." The answer you receive may make you a little nervous because intuition often suggests you do something out of your comfort zone. Still, you'll experience a "rightness" about it.

Not Your Average Coin-Toss Technique

This is a great technique to use when you'd like to move out of your comfort zone. I wouldn't necessarily use this method for major decisions like whether to get divorced, quit your job, or move across the continent. But then that's just me!

Think about a decision you're trying to make. Form it in your mind as a yes-or-no question. Examples are: "Is this the right exercise plan for me?" "Is this the right time to ask for a raise?" "Is it important that I attend the annual association meeting next month?"

Take a coin and flip it. Heads indicates yes. Tails indicates no. Okay, what was the answer?

Think about how you felt about the answer. Were you disappointed? Relieved? Did you get a thrill of excitement through your body, or a knot of fear in your stomach? Admit it, did you immediately want to flip the coin two more times and try for best two out of three? (Or have you actually done that already?)

Any of these responses is an example of your intuition speaking to you. You know the answer. It's the one you wanted in the first place. Your response after you tossed the coin gave you more information about the answer to your question.

So often we expect our intuition to speak like Darth Vader in Star Wars booming out, "Yes! Take that job!" It's more likely that the message will come through subtle feelings, an inner nudge, a physical sensation. When you learn to pay attention to these inner clues and act on them, you can expect your decision making to become more successful.

Once you make a decision,
the universe conspires to make it happen.
—RALPH WALDO EMERSON

YOUR INTUITION JOURNAL

A Mind Map is a helpful technique to try when you want to gain insight about a particular problem or issue. On a blank page in your journal, ask a question about a decision you're trying to make.

In the space below the question, jot down any words or images that come to mind about this issue. Do this for ten minutes adding more words, pictures, or symbols as they come to you.

The words and images don't need to make sense to your logical mind. Don't judge it, simply write it or draw it.

When you've exhausted your list of ideas (or your ten minutes is up), go back and circle any images or words that produce an aha feeling or a sense of excitement.

Is there any action you feel compelled to take right now? If not, trust that the exercise has stimulated your intuition, which will want to serve up more possibilities for you. Pay attention to any new ideas that emerge throughout the day(s) after you try this technique. Write down any and all answers that come to you.

CHAPTER 21

The Art of Surrender

God, grant me the serenity to accept the things
I cannot change, the courage to change the things
I can and the wisdom to know the difference.
—REINHOLD NIEBUHR

The day is emblazoned in my memory. I was twenty-eight years old. My boyfriend of six months, whom I was convinced was "The One," had unceremoniously dumped me the previous week. I was feeling alone and quite desperate for a committed relationship. It was a life dream to get married and have a family. I wanted to be a mom. The biological clock was ticking . . . or so I thought.

I had an appointment that Friday afternoon with an endocrinologist. My regular doctor had noted some hormone imbalances that he felt should be investigated more fully. Going to see the specialist was the last thing I felt like doing, but it had taken four months to get in to see the guy. Besides, I wasn't doing anything except sitting home and crying over my lost love. At least a visit with the doctor was a distraction.

I hadn't really expected a whole lot. I had been experiencing irregular periods for a while. Perhaps the doctor would order some more tests or give me some medicine to take. I was ushered into the physician's office fairly quickly. I was surprised it wasn't an exam room. He was seated behind a huge mahogany desk and looked like a man who didn't want to waste time—mine or his. He shook my hand and with his other hand grabbed some papers off his desk and pushed them toward me.

"I'd like you to look at these," he said. I could see they were lab results but beyond that they didn't have any significance to me. I had no idea what I was looking at or how to interpret the information on the sheet in front of me. I looked at the numbers and looked back at him. It was at that point he said the words that changed my life. "Obviously it shows you're infertile. You can't have children."

I actually thought I had misheard him. Could he have just said what I thought he did? I was totally unprepared for this. I couldn't believe he would deliver sensitive information like this so callously. I must have stared at him with a blank look because he just repeated what he'd already said, "No children for you. You and your husband will have to adopt."

Usually I'm fairly quick coming up with questions and responding in a crisis. This time I felt like someone had put fog in my brain. I couldn't form a thought other than that I wanted to get out of there and away from this insensitive jerk before I started sobbing hysterically. I managed a small, "Oh!" and "Thank you," before darting out of the room.

I don't remember driving home. I managed to keep myself together as I maneuvered through Boston's infamous rush-hour traffic. However, once I got to my apartment, I couldn't stop crying. I went through a box of tissues while sitting curled up on my sofa. Hours went by as I sat there thinking about the consequences of what the doctor had said.

At around 11:00 p.m. I called a couple of close friends. I got their answering machines and imagined them out with their husbands enjoying wedded bliss. I thought about calling another friend who was six months' pregnant but the thought of speaking to her about this was just too painful. I finally fell asleep at midnight only to wake up two hours later.

Near 2:00 a.m. I felt even more distraught and scared. I burst into a fresh round of crying and then decided to pray. "Dear God. I don't know what to do. I really want a marriage and children. I surrender this situation to you. Please give me a sign that all will be well and that I'll be able to have a family."

The phone rang. It was 2:00 a.m. Who calls at 2:00 a.m.?! I picked up the phone and said "Hello." There was a short pause. An intake of breath and then the person on the other end said . . . "Hello. Mom?"

It was a young girl calling home. At first I couldn't speak. Then I said, "Honey. You have the right wrong number. Hang up and try your mom again. I'm sure you'll reach her this time."

I hung up and sat there staring at the phone. It was as if I'd received a call from God Himself. It was then that I understood the true power of surrender.

Now, I can't report to you that all my subsequent attempts at surrendering were met with such an obvious and quick response. But I continue to be in awe of the miracles that can happen when I've released the outcome of a situation and invited God in to provide a solution.

Several years after this event, I met and married my husband, Gary. I became the proud stepmom to his then seven-year-old son, Cliff. I am grateful to report Gary and I have been happily together for almost twenty years. Cliff is now twenty-seven and I'm still a proud stepmom. God kept his promise.

Most people begin a personal relationship with God when something forces them to surrender. You've tried everything that you can think of to fix a bad marriage, get out of debt, find a job, or heal your body from an illness or accident. You may have given up on yourself, but God hasn't given up on you. It's time for letting go and letting miracles happen.

One of my clients, Jeff, lost his wife after a car accident in which he was driving. For almost a year he repeated this scene endlessly in his mind, replaying the icy conditions, the loss of control of their car, the sickening thud as the passenger side of the car hit the tree, followed by viewing his wife's lifeless body. Jeff went to therapy, tried antidepressants, and talked with friends and anyone else who would listen. He was inconsolable.

His life had become an endless series of if-onlys—if only he had done this or hadn't done that. He realized he wasn't honoring the relationship he'd had with his wife and their children by staying in his suffering. One day in prayer, he asked God to "take this burden from me." He missed his wife terribly and yet he felt he needed to rejoin the human race and forgive himself.

Jeff said, "The emotional pain didn't end immediately as I said this prayer of surrendering. I simply found that little by little I came to an acceptance. It was as if a small slice of light entered my previously darkened fortress. As each day passed, I continued giving the situation over to God and asking for help. That slice of light became a little wider. I released my wife's memory into God's hands and opened myself up to forgiveness. It was a slow journey of acceptance and recovery, but the turning point came when I surrendered."

Like Jeff, I've discovered that when I find the simple grace to accept what is and cease struggling, I can allow miracles to happen. Surrender is not passive. It's about releasing what's not working in our lives and asking for God's guidance and direction. It requires faith and trust. Our task is to open up, accept the wisdom and opportunities that come our way, and act on them.

As human beings we are wired for wisdom and guidance from God. When we learn how to listen to our intuition, we will hear the guidance that will direct us to our next step. We don't have to be concerned with all the details about how to reach our goals and visions. We only need to be concerned about listening for the next steps.

You have probably read the words "Let go and let God" many times. And you've probably asked yourself, "What is this surrender thing all about? Does it mean that I have no role or responsibility for action in this process?" Letting it go to God always sounded so passive to me. It used to scare me more than help me. I thought of it as giving up on what I wanted or waving a proverbial "white flag" of surrender. But it's not that at all.

To trust in God is to believe that there is a friendly, abundant, loving, wise energy in the Universe that supports you and wants what's best for you. It supports your highest good. Letting your fears, concerns, wishes, prayers "go to God" means that you trust and work with this energy that powers the universe. God will work with you through your own built-in guidance system to help draw to you what you want.

If you or a loved one has been involved in a 12-step program such as Alcoholics or Gamblers Anonymous, you know about the power of surrender. The third step is "to turn our will and our lives over to the care of our Higher Power." There is huge power when you combine that with the eleventh step, to seek "through prayer and meditation to improve our conscious contact with our Higher Power, praying only for knowledge of our Higher Power's will for us and the power to carry that out."

But how do you "let go" or "go with the flow"? I sometimes wish I could buy a Surrender Switch to let me know I had switched on that flow! I'm most comfortable when I'm taking action on something. The concept of seeming to do nothing except "let go to God" has been a tough one to get my head around! Here's the technique I use when I've been struggling with an issue with no results. I call it the Surrender Box.

The Surrender Box Technique

Write out your worry or concern on a three-by-five card or slip of paper. For example: "Dear God, I'm having a difficult time communicating with my husband about our marriage. I want to feel close to him again. Everything I've tried hasn't worked. I am surrendering this concern to you and ask for wise guidance to bring about a positive result."

Summarize your concern with a question. "How can I develop a loving, close partnership with my husband?"

Close your eyes and go to a place of peace inside you. Take a few slow deep breaths until you feel your energy begin to shift. Call God to you. Imagine being in the presence of incredible love and wisdom.

Repeat the concern that you've written on the paper. Ask your question. Listen for any words, feelings, images, or sudden insights. Maintain a respectful silence, allowing any wisdom to emerge into your consciousness. Sometimes a new option will emerge out of the quiet. When you feel ready, imagine placing this concern in a bubble of light or see it being released to God in some other form. Know that you will receive further information to help you resolve this issue.

After you've finished your meditation, place your card in a box and put it on a shelf where you will see it frequently. I decorated my box and wrote the word surrender on it. When you find yourself beginning to worry about this issue at any point in the day or night, remind yourself that you have let go of this concern and that you will receive guidance to resolve it. I like this technique because the tangible fact of placing the issue in a box helps me remember that I've surrendered it.

Your only other task is to be open to receiving guidance. You listen for this inner wisdom on a daily basis. You'll find yourself being given one step at a time. The answer may come through an inspired idea, a dream, or a fleeting insight that opens your mind to a new direction. When you consistently look within, asking "What is the right course of action?" or "What path should I take?"—you'll be rewarded with wise guidance. It will always be there gracing your steps through life. You'll find that your fear begins to drop away and you'll move forward with confidence.

A Prayer of Surrender

When I am stuck in anger, fear, or some other strong emotion, unable to let go of a situation, I remember Luke 22:42: "Father, if it is Your will, take this cup from me; yet not my will but Yours be done." I have a prayer of surrender that helps me find peace: "God, please help me release my fear about this situation and let it go to you. I ask for your peace. I ask for your wisdom in my mind, in my heart, and on my lips. Give me the strength, vision, and courage to understand and do your will. Show me the path that leads to the greatest good for all concerned. Amen."

Accepting What Is

"Acceptance of what has happened is the first step in overcoming the consequence of any misfortune," wrote the philosopher William James. Is there something you need to accept today, right now? What if you knew deep in your soul that all is well? Your life is as it needs to be in this moment. You're okay.

Life may not be what you want, but perhaps you can entertain the idea that you have what you need. Contemplate the idea that you are centered in Spirit and there is absolutely nothing to fix or to change.

> Acceptance of what has happened is the first step in overcoming the consequence of any misfortune.

Surrender the need to fix your life, the situation you're in, or the world in general. Life is what it is for now. In the next moment, wisdom comes, love enters and you are presented with the perfect solution. It's still all perfect, and so are you.

Faith means being grasped by a power that is greater than we are, a power that shakes us and turns us, and transforms and heals us. Surrendering to this power is faith.
—Paul Tillich

YOUR INTUITION JOURNAL

Here are some questions to contemplate. Note the answers you receive in your journal.

- How can you invite faith to play a larger role in your life in the days ahead?

- Can you remember a time in the past when you let go of the outcome of a situation? What happened?

- What technique would work for you to help you surrender a particular struggle you're currently experiencing?

CHAPTER 22

What's Your Calling?

Where your talents and the needs of the
world cross lies your calling.
—ARISTOTLE

"What's my life purpose?" "What's my mission?" "What am I supposed to do with my life?" "How can I find some clarity so I know what to do?" These are questions I frequently hear from people whose lives have been turned upside down. The subject arises not just from people who have lost their jobs. An illness may make you unable to go back to your former career. A divorce may force you to support yourself and your kids for the first time in your life. The death of a loved one may compel you to search for a deeper meaning and a desire to contribute to the world in a different way.

Whatever the reason, you may suddenly find yourself seeking your calling. Joseph Jaworski wrote in his book *Synchronicity,* "I discovered that people are not really afraid of dying; they're afraid of not ever having lived, not ever having deeply considered their life's higher purpose, and not ever having stepped into that purpose and at least tried to make a difference in this world."

At the depth of any crisis, we seek purpose and meaning. We find ourselves compelled to follow some inner instinct that says, "Yes. There is a reason for all of this." We desperately seek the answer in the hope of finding direction. Perhaps the thing that you've always felt was a failure in your life becomes the very thing that leads to your success.

> . . .people are not really afraid of dying; they're afraid of not ever having lived . . .

I had a client who was fired from a job more than a year ago. She felt terrible about it and was quite worried that life, as she knew it, was over. I saw her again recently and she described a new job and career in glowing terms. She had found her bliss! She told me she would have never left her old job if left to her own decision. The life crisis had turned into a life blessing.

Listening for the Call

It would be wonderful if each of our life crises came with a script or some instruction book that tells us what we are meant to learn, or do, or become. In the Bible, God spoke to Moses through a burning bush. He wanted Moses to be the leader of the Israelites. That was how Moses received his calling. I don't know about you, but if God began speaking to me from burning bushes, I'd probably run in the other direction while questioning my sanity.

So how do the rest of us mere mortals receive instruction and direction to help us find our way? God speaks to us in many ways. You come to this life with specific talents, aptitudes, interests, and abilities. Through your inner guidance you begin to understand and use these gifts.

You come here with an assignment, or a life purpose, if you will. It may be the task of raising a family, transforming a business, communicating your ideas as a teacher, or being a leader in your community. Your task may be a massive one such as raising the level of constructive communication between warring countries, or awakening a consciousness of love and forgiveness in a segment of the population. Whatever purpose your soul has come to address, your intuition will give you the guidance and life experiences necessary to fulfill it.

Many people assume this life purpose is a job or career. But our purpose is not necessarily a thing we need to do; it may be a quality we need to develop in order for our soul to unfold and grow to the next level. Through an illness you might learn to let others help you or, conversely, learn self-reliance. You may have grown up with an alcoholic parent and learned about empathy and forgiveness. Through the death of a child we may find love and compassion, and awaken the ability to connect to our spirituality.

The call of your life purpose comes in many disguises. These disguises may provide only partial answers. But like a divining rod, they at least show you where to dig. These include:

- Something you love to do in your free time
- An interest you had as a child
- An issue or subject you feel strongly about
- A dream that keeps recurring
- Words, phrases, images that arise out of meditation or prayer
- An observation that people frequently make about you
- A strong inclination to "make a difference" in the world
- A life lesson you repeatedly have to learn and want to help others who are also struggling
- Something that is so much fun you'd do it without being paid for it

I can think of many clients over the last twenty-five years who have turned a passion into a calling. One of my favorite stories is of Rita, who turned a ho-hum job as an office manager into a profitable calling and had fun doing it.

Rita had a one-word answer when I asked her what she loved to do in her spare time: "Shop!" She explained that she was fascinated by fashion, color, and fabric and enjoyed helping her girlfriends buy new clothes each season. Her family had lived on welfare through most of her childhood, and the idea of having the abundance to shop for things she and her friends enjoyed was a great pleasure. She had also entertained the idea of becoming a social worker to encourage women who were raised in similar circumstances find jobs.

How did Rita resolve these two disparate interests and discover her calling? She became a certified image consultant working with corporate women who needed help projecting the right fashion image for their work. In her free time she counseled and mentored women coming off welfare and interviewing for their first jobs. She also created a storefront "closet" of wonderful and expensive clothing that were castoffs from her image consulting clients and gave them to her welfare clients to wear to their interviews and subsequent jobs. It was a win–win for everyone.

Finding Your Calling

Here is a list of sentence completion statements designed to help point you in the direction of your calling. The best way to fill them out is by doing them quickly. Don't think about them too much. If you get stuck on one, skip it and go back to it later.

As a child, I loved to _____.

I've always wanted to _____.

*One of my favorite things to do when I have free time is*_____
_____.

I feel most alive when _____.

People often tell me _____.

The thing I do effortlessly is _____.

I love to read or learn about _____.

A perfect day would be _____.

If money were no object, I would _____.

I've always dreamed of _____.

I have always struggled with _____.

If I could make the world a better place, I would _____.

If my fairy godmother could wave her magic wand over me and proclaim my ideal life, I would describe it this way: _____
_____.

One of the people I most admire is _____.
and the reason I admire her/him is _____.

I'm truly happy when I'm _____.

I've noticed synchronicities and coincidences that seem to point me in the direction of _____.

The one thing that needs to change in my life in order for me to do what I love is _____.

I secretly believe my life purpose is _____ *but I allow* _____ *to stand in my way.*

In order to begin living my life purpose I need to _____.

I am committed to living my purpose. This week I will _____ _____ *as a step towards honoring my calling.*

The thing that most surprised me as I was completing these sentences is _____.

If I could summarize my life purpose, I would state it this way:

_____.

We both know that a sentence completion exercise in a book is not going to speak to you as strongly as God's voice from a burning bush. But it's a start. So . . . what did you learn about yourself? If you're like most people, you'll finish the sentences and begin an internal dialogue that will immediately tell you all the reasons you can't do what you love. But what if you can?

Here's where your intuition comes in. I'd like you to begin to entertain the idea that it is possible to begin living your purpose. Instead of the constantly running voice of defeat in your head telling you "I don't know what to do," "Other people know this stuff, but I don't," "I'm so confused," "I couldn't make money at this," or whatever else your defeatist voice says, listen to a different voice.

What if I did know what to do?

How could I make a living at this?

What would my life look like if I were doing what I love instead of what I hate?

What next steps could I take?

Let me be open to new possibilities. (This is my all-time favorite statement when faced with uncertainty.)

I think that perhaps God has moved from talking to us from burning bushes to something equally as powerful—our inner wisdom. Jon Kabat-Zinn wrote in his book, *Wherever You Go, There You Are,* "It is useful at times to admit you don't know your way and to be open to help from unexpected places." The answers may not pop into your mind fully formed, but as you begin to ask the right questions you'll be led, step by step, in the direction of your calling.

Be Open to Divine Nudges

My friend Barbara was in a dead-end job at a local university. The administration had decided to shut down her department and was slowly laying off the staff. She longed for a job that both paid her well and put her marketing and public relations skills to use in a service-oriented company she could believe in. One evening on a whim, she attended a lecture by the founder of a new kind of assisted living center. She loved the ideas he put forth about a vibrant place filled with culture, learning, and fun activities.

I remember her saying she would love to work at a place like that. She was so moved by his vision of this center that she wrote him a personal thank-you note. She included some marketing ideas that came to her during his talk. Several days later she was surprised to receive a call from him. They had a position open for someone with her skills. Would she be interested in coming in for an interview? She's been there almost a year now and it's been a dream come true. Her whim (or intuition) paid off for her in a big way, pointing her in the direction of her calling.

What about you? Have you been paying attention to or ignoring the Divine nudges encouraging you to check out a new direction? A nudge is defined as a "gentle push." We often receive these when we're a bit off course in life, not following our callings, or out of sync with our greater purpose. When we don't pay attention to the nudges, the Universe generally ups the ante. The nudges are followed by an escalating series of shoves, bumps, and prods proceeded by all-out chaos.

The following is not meant to be a definitive statement on a specific action to take if you're receiving a Divine nudge. It's there to get you thinking about alternatives to inaction.

The Nudge	Possible Action Steps
You're bored with what you currently do for work.	Take a course in something you're interested in. Talk to people who are doing work you might enjoy.
You're so overwhelmed you can't begin to formulate any ideas about your life's purpose.	It may be time to let go of something. What's draining you? Who is draining you? What projects or commitments can you release?
You have lots of ideas of things you like to do and that excite you. You simply find that you talk yourself out of them before you begin.	Take the attitude that you're simply gathering information. You don't have to make a decision right now. Take a small next step. It doesn't have to be a leap.
Other people constantly talk you out of your hopes and dreams.	Ask yourself, "What is true for me?" Begin to surround yourself with people who are doers rather than naysayers.
You know you have to change but don't have a clue where to begin.	Begin to ask yourself, "What would be fun today?" or "What would be interesting?" You don't have to make a decision about the rest of your life. Just practice with one day at a time.

You consistently stop yourself from dreaming big dreams because you don't have money, support, or something else that seems to stand in your way.	God can work miracles. Whenever the defeatist thoughts begin, replace them with "Let me be open to possibilities." Pay attention to any synchronicities, coincidences, or nudges that lead you in a new direction.
My life feels too small for me. I dream of doing something bigger, more profound. I want to be of service.	Be willing to move out of your comfort zone. Take some risks. Do something that compels you or interests you even if it doesn't make sense.

A chapter of a few hundred words cannot delve into this topic of life purpose deeply enough. If you want to read more, one of the best books on the subject is *Callings: Finding and Following an Authentic Life* by Gregg Levoy. He wrote, "'What do you love?' As you listen for callings keep such a question in your mind to help tune out some of the static. In fact, 'What do you love' is the question that callings pose."

There is rarely a moment in life where you'll say, "This is it! This is my life purpose!" More likely you'll uncover it over a period of time, in a series of stops and starts. It will reveal itself as you trust your intuition and take steps both small and large to move out of the comfort zone of the familiar. It's normal to feel uncertain, to retreat and then proceed. It's like the "hot and cold" game you may have played as a kid. Your intuition will send up clues that you're getting closer (hot) or moving away (cold) from your purpose by how you feel and the results you achieve.

Begin to keep track of all the intuitive signals you've been receiving. Don't dismiss them out of hand. Pay attention to the daydreams, fantasies, interests, and coincidences you may have been experiencing. What's on your bookshelf that fascinates you? What do you clip out of the newspaper to read more thoroughly? What opportunities are showing up in your life? What quotes do you have tacked up on your fridge? These are all hints and clues that will help you unfold the mystery of your calling.

When you know your life purpose, you tap into a source of power that enables you to achieve your goals more easily and effectively. Susan

Jeffers, the author of *Feel the Fear and Do It Anyway,* wrote, "We become powerful in the face of our fears when we have a sense that we make a difference in this world." As your purpose in life evolves, you'll find yourself with more clarity, energy, and abundance.

To the degree we're each waiting for word
of our callings, we ought to tend the soul of silence.
We need to teach ourselves to sit quietly and listen,
just listen, long enough to leave a decent
indentation on the couch.
—GREGG LEVOY

YOUR INTUITION JOURNAL

Review the sentence completion statements under the "Finding Your Calling" section in this chapter. Which ones leaped out at you? What are the top five that you found compelling? That's your intuition trying to get your attention.

Copy those five into your journal and spend some time writing about the answers.

CHAPTER 23

What Dreams May Come

Dreams are my compass and my truth;
they guide me and link me to the divine.
—JUDITH ORLOFF

Dreams can provide you with a wealth of information and insight when you're struggling with a challenging decision or a major life event. My client Yuka, who lives in Tokyo, told me she had been offered a job in the city of Kyoto. She had written numerous pro and con lists about accepting the job and she was still woefully undecided. She was leaning toward taking the offer but still had a somewhat negative feeling about it. She asked for a dream to help her gain clarity. (I share her technique in the "Sleep on It" section that follows.)

She told me she awoke the next morning with vivid recall of a dream in which there was a big sign by the side of the road that said "kyoto 368km" (about 220 miles). The thing that intrigued her and made her decide not to accept the job offer was the fact that there was also a huge stop sign that towered over the Kyoto sign.

Yuka turned down the Kyoto job and the following week interviewed for a position within a Tokyo company that was a perfect match for her skills, talents, and interests. They offered her more money as well as a better title—and best of all she didn't have to make the move away from family and friends. She was relieved she'd listened to the guidance in her dream.

Wouldn't it be wonderful if all dreams were so clear and direct? Usually if you can remember them at all, they're filled with random images, scenes, and symbols. You wake up scratching your head in the morning, wondering what was going on while you were sleeping. However, you spend about a third of your life asleep, so wouldn't it be great to use this time to your advantage?

You can, in fact, receive a lot of guidance from your dreams with only a small amount of effort. It's fertile territory for wisdom from your intuition. You only have to ask and listen. You can expect the answers will come, and with practice your dream images and symbols will begin to make sense to you. You can receive answers to questions about relationships, career, spiritual direction, moneymaking ideas, inventions, and your health, to name but a few.

Dreams can also provide intuitive nudges that tell you when you're off track in your life. For example, a dream I've had at times throughout my life is one where I'm living alone in a tiny, unfurnished apartment. I know that when I have that dream, it's my intuition telling me I'm isolating myself too much. It's time to call some friends, have fun, and get out of my office!

Sleep on It

Suppose you could go to sleep at night and wake up with solutions to any problem you're currently experiencing. The requirements? Just a nice soft bed, a little thinking and writing, a pad and pencil on the nightstand. After that you just close your eyes and dream. All you need to do upon awakening is be willing to write down your insights. That's it! Need more detail? Here are some steps you can take to use your sleep time to resolve problems and come up with creative solutions:

1. Write Down the Problem in a Dream Journal

This doesn't need to be anything fancy. A notebook or pad of paper beside your bed works great. If you're not concerned with waking a bedmate, a recorder could work as well. Before you go to sleep, write a few paragraphs about the decision you're trying to make or the issue you're seeking insight about. It could be as simple as, "I'm really worried about my job. I think my company may be downsizing. I need to make money and I'd like to continue working in my same field and not have to make a geographic move."

2. Summarize the Issue

Read the paragraph(s) you've written and condense it into a one-sentence question. I like questions that evoke more than a yes or no answer. For example: "What's the next step I need to take regarding my career?" "How can I find a fun, interesting, and well-paid job?" "What should I do regarding my career?" Others have found it easier to simply ask for information about a concern. "I need information about a new career direction." "I would like a dream about a prosperous and fun new career."

3. Ask the Question or State the Concern as You Drift Off to Sleep

Tell yourself that you'll remember a dream that will provide the answer(s) to this question. As you doze off, repeat your phrase softly to yourself, with the mental expectation of receiving an answer. If your mind wanders, gently bring it back to the question.

4. Wake Up Slowly

As you wake up, try not to come fully awake at first. Ask yourself, "Did I have a dream about my concern?" Don't get out of bed. In fact, move as little as possible when you're in the middle of dream recall. Just lie there for a few minutes, retrieving your dream images.

5. Record the Dreams or Dream Fragments

Even if you don't remember the entire dream, jot down the fragments. Answers in dreams don't always announce themselves in an obvious way. They'll show up through symbolic images, metaphors, feelings, and sensations. Your dream recall may not happen as soon as you wake up. You may find pieces of it coming back to you throughout your day. For this reason, it's helpful to keep your notebook nearby.

6. Interpret the Dream

There are vast libraries of books on the subject of dream interpretation. However, many tend to reduce everything to a universal symbol. You are the best interpreter of your dreams. For example, a fire might signify a romantic evening to one person, but to you it might be a sign of danger. Here are some items to consider to help you jump-start your interpretation.

Look for the solution.

Is there an immediate answer you've received upon awakening? Perhaps you didn't even remember a dream, but woke up with an answer or idea. That's perfectly okay. If you did recall a dream, what can you take away from it that would be helpful in your current situation? Is there any part of your dream that leaps out at you as important and worthy of some further reflection?

Identify the symbols.

Are there dream symbols or metaphors that pertain to your question from the night before? How might these be relevant to your question and answer? What pops into your mind when you think about these symbols? Who or what in your life do they remind you of? If there are people who appear in your dream, what might they represent or symbolize? A client described a dream where she had been planting bulbs and then watching as they grew, poking up quickly through the soil. It resonated with her as symbolic of the rapid changes she had experienced in her own life, and she felt comforted by the dream.

Describe the dream out loud.

A dream's meaning may become clear when you verbalize it, because we often use plays on words to form pictures. For example, I once had a dream about a pain in my foot. I kept saying, "It hurts to put my foot down." I realized I was unconsciously referring to my inability to "put my foot down" in a situation with a colleague at work. You might also describe your dream in the first person, present tense. This will often evoke some overlooked piece of information.

Create a dream symbol notebook.

If your dreams are presenting you with themes or symbols that frequently reappear, you might want to create a chart or notebook about them. For each recurring symbol answer the following questions:

- What feeling do you associate with the symbol?
- When you visualize the image, what immediately pops into your mind?

Imagine yourself being the symbolic dream image and speaking in the first person. For instance, if you have a dream that involves a lion at the zoo, you as the lion might say, "I feel trapped and confined. I want to break free." While it may feel odd to become an inanimate or animate object in your dream, it can spark an intuitive insight.

Ask simply, "What does this symbol represent?" If you find yourself getting anything from a "zing" of recognition to feeling a bit teary, you'll know you hit on the right interpretation.

Also think about whether a pun could be associated with this image. (For example; sun = son; coin = change.) If you relate to the "pun factor" in dreams, you'll love this old joke: "A guy goes to a psychiatrist. Doc, I keep having these alternating recurring dreams. First I'm a tepee, then I'm a wigwam, then I'm a tepee, then I'm a wigwam. It's driving me crazy. What's wrong with me?"

The doctor replies, "Isn't it obvious? You're too tense." (Two tents.)

Your Personal Dream Analyst

Carl Jung was a Swiss psychiatrist, an influential thinker, and the founder of analytical psychology. He emphasized the importance of balance and harmony. He believed that we rely too heavily on science and logic and would benefit from integrating spirituality and appreciation of unconscious realms.

When Jung interpreted dreams, he would ask his patients questions about the images in their dreams. From these questions, he asked them to discuss all of the associations that came to mind. Here are the questions:

- What is the shape of the image?
- What is the function of the image?
- What alterations does the image go through?
- What does the image do?

- What do you like and dislike about the image?
- What does the image remind you of?

Jung had a great deal of confidence in the individual's unconscious wisdom. He believed that dream images are attempts by the unconscious to communicate with the conscious self. The dreamer was encouraged to brainstorm all the different symbolic associations for each aspect of the dream.

As an example, say a dream included birds. Possible associations with this symbol include flight, freedom, and cages. Another aspect of Jungian dream analysis is active imagination. Here, the dreamer mentally evokes a character from the dream and asks it questions.

Suggestions for Recalling Your Dreams

Some people tell me they never remember their dreams. They've found it helpful to repeat what I call a dream-recall mantra before drifting off to sleep. It might be as simple as breathing slowly in and out while saying, "Tonight I will remember my dreams," or "I'm looking forward to seeing what my dreams reveal."

Visualization helps, too. One woman simply drifted off to sleep visualizing herself writing in her dream journal and saying, "I learn so much from my dreams!" For others, it may simply take a few weeks of establishing the ritual of asking your pre-sleep questions and keeping pen and paper on the bedside table. After some practice, you should find that you can recall at least three dreams a week.

Before you go to sleep:
- Tell yourself you'll remember your dreams.
- Review your dream journal from the previous few days.
- Have your pen and paper ready.
- Ask your dream question.

Upon waking:
- Wake gently.
- Try to remember all the dreams you can, even the dream fragments.

- Don't be discouraged if you have no recall.
- Write it down! Don't just tell yourself you'll remember.

Dream Money

A few months after I was married to my husband, Gary, I decided to ask my dream for a way to create more abundance. I had moved into his small ranch house, and we wanted to enlarge it by renovating and adding a second floor. This was going to cost a fair amount of money.

On a Tuesday night I used the dream technique I described above. I woke up early Wednesday morning with six numbers running through my head. I found I could neither fall back to sleep nor stop the numbers from endlessly repeating themselves in my mind.

I had never played a lottery before, but it occurred to me that these numbers might represent a lottery win. Gary was snoring softly beside me. I shook him gently and said, "How many numbers are in the Massachusetts state lottery?"

"Six," came his mumbled response.

"I think I might have the winning lottery number," I replied.

He was on his feet in a second, grabbed a paper and pen, and was ready to write down the numbers before I barely had the words out of my mouth. I'd never seen him wake up that fast!

With the "winning numbers" in hand, Gary agreed to play them in the Wednesday lottery. I promptly put the whole thing out of my mind until Friday morning when I casually asked if he'd checked on whether our number had won.

He confessed that he had a crisis at work and had forgotten to play the game on Wednesday, but hastened to add that he had placed bets for both Thursday and Friday.

We took out the newspaper to find the lottery list. You guessed it . . . My numbers were the winning numbers for Wednesday! The same day I received the information and the day he didn't play it. We would have won $5.2 million.

Sigh . . . So close, yet so far away . . .

Yes. I am still married to him. I also have a very long list of people who have volunteered to be called if I come up with another winning number. So far, it hasn't happened again.

What did I learn from this? A couple of things. One, it's a good story to tell when someone asks me, "If you're so intuitive, why haven't you won the lottery?" (I hate that question!) And two, it's not enough to simply receive intuitive information, you also have to act on it.

Your vision will become clear only when you look into your heart. Who looks outside, dreams. Who looks inside, awakens.
—CARL GUSTAV JUNG

YOUR INTUITION JOURNAL

Write down your dream question in your notebook before you turn off the light and lie down.

Keep the pad of paper and pen beside your bed.

When you awaken, write any dreams or dream fragments that you remember.

CHAPTER 24

Are You Stuck in a Rut and Can't Get Up?

Action may not always bring happiness;
but there is no happiness without action.
—BENJAMIN DISRAELI

"I feel stuck." "I'm in a rut." "I don't like where I am but I don't know what to do." Those are words I hear frequently from clients. Life feels stalled. All those big hopes and dreams you once had for yourself seem like they're on a distant horizon or even in another universe altogether.

Jenny was one of those people. She'd taken a job right out of college. It wasn't in her area of interest, but she considered herself lucky to have work and be reasonably well paid. The problem was that she was bored with what she was doing and saw no prospects for change.

I'm one of these people who have just fallen into things. I chose my college because my best friend was going there. I chose my major simply because it was considered an easy course. My job is a "good enough" job but doesn't require creativity or a great deal of intelligence.

I'm thirty-four years old and it's finally occurred to me to ask myself, "What do I really want and what would excite me?" I just feel stuck. Frankly, I think I've gotten so out of the habit of challenging myself. It's like an underutilized muscle. I need to get it stimulated and strong so I can take a stand in my life. But where do I begin to look?

Trust Your Intuition

Intuition is an infallible guide for letting you know when you need a change and also what direction to take. Here's an easy way to think about it:

If you feel excited, interested, and/or passionate about something, that's your intuition saying, "Go in that direction."

Conversely, if you feel bored, uninterested, and/or drained by something, that's your intuition communicating that change is needed. "Go in a new direction."

Jenny was getting the message loud and clear that she needed a change. How about you? Here's a list of questions to ask yourself.

Are You Ready for a Change?

	Yes	No
I want to be in a different job next year.	☐	☐
I like my career, but feel I'm in the wrong position.	☐	☐
I long for the weekends when I can work on my hobbies or other interests.	☐	☐
There are other career choices that have always fascinated me and I'd like to check them out.	☐	☐
I need to find something new that's fresh and creative.	☐	☐
I feel I've done everything I can to change a bad relationship. I'm convinced it won't get better and yet I can't seem to leave.	☐	☐
I spin my wheels and don't know where to begin.	☐	☐
My work has become predictable and boring.	☐	☐
I have other interests but I never or rarely pursue them.	☐	☐
I hardly ever have time for creative or spiritual pursuits.	☐	☐
I find myself daydreaming a lot about switching careers.	☐	☐
I don't like where I am in life, but I don't know what I want, either.	☐	☐
I think about change, but I get stuck in inaction.	☐	☐
I feel excited about a new career direction but can't figure out a way to earn a living at it.	☐	☐

I long for a way to make a contribution to my community but don't feel I can do it in my present work.	☐	☐
My life feels out of balance. (Too much work and not enough family, social, and personal time.)	☐	☐
I'd like to move, but I don't know where I'd go.	☐	☐
I'm ready to work for myself. (Or, if you're already an entrepreneur:) I'm ready to work for someone else.	☐	☐

If you answered yes to most of the questions, you're definitely in a rut. Your intuition is telling you unambiguously that it's time for a change. If you're not clear about your goals, your objective should be to become clear. Begin to think about what's interesting to you and what you can let go of in order to make room for something new.

Jenny admitted that she was stuck in that limbo period between "I know it's time to change my work" and "I don't know what I want to do next." It's an unsettling time for most people. We hate not knowing. The famous philosopher "Anonymous" once said, "The bend in the road is not the end of the road unless you refuse to make the turn." Here are some steps to get you started so you can make the right turn:

Acknowledge it's time for a change.

You don't need to give up a job, career, or relationship right now as the result of this insight. Just let yourself get used to the idea that you want to change and you're simply exploring new directions. Consider letting

> The bend in the road is not the end of the road unless you refuse to make the turn.

friends and appropriate colleagues know what you're thinking and feeling. They may see that you possess strengths, skills, and interests that you haven't acknowledged in yourself. They also could provide some insight about what's been keeping you stuck.

Jenny felt that simply stating that she was ready for a change was extremely empowering for her. While she still didn't know what life might bring, she felt excited about it for the first time in a long time.

Give yourself a period of time to gather information.

Depending on your situation, this can be a few weeks to a few years. You're using this time to consult your inner compass, your intuition. Of the possibilities in front of you, what feels exciting? Be willing to explore interests that may not make immediate sense. An example might be taking a class on something you're interested in or volunteering with a group that's a bit outside your comfort zone. Within your dreams, interests, and aspirations you'll find opportunity. It's as if your intuition gives you clues about the best path to follow even though your limited logical mind may not know where you're headed!

Jenny took classes in jewelry making, small-business marketing, Spanish, and "How to Start a Pet-Sitting Business." She told me that the classes got her out of the house, into new situations, and began to open her mind to her creative side as well as the possibility of starting her own business. "Also, I was with so many new people. I began to see myself differently through their eyes. I realized I had a lot of strengths and talents I hadn't recognized before."

Commit to taking action steps.

Motivational speaker and author Tony Robbins once observed, "You see, in life, lots of people know what to do, but few people actually do what they know. Knowing is not enough! You must take action." What are three things you could do this month that would give you information about your interest? Perhaps you could research it on the Web, read a book, make an appointment with a career coach, or talk to someone who has a similar goal. It doesn't have to be a huge risk. When you commit to action, your intuition can begin to guide you. It puts options, possibility, and hope in your path.

Ask your intuition open-ended questions.

These might include "What would I enjoy doing for work?" "What next steps can I take that will lead me in the right direction?" "Who can I talk with that will help me with these choices?" "What could I do that would help others and be fun for me?" As you go about your day, pay attention to any inner nudges or impulses from your intuition that point you in a new direction.

Jenny told me that this was all new to her. She'd never asked herself what she really wanted. "I was always taught to just be grateful for anything that came my way. This idea of personal choice helped me more than anything. I kept asking myself, 'What would be fun today?' I found out I liked to have fun as well as be creative!"

Stop saying, "I don't know" and "I'm stuck."
There is part of you that does know, and it's providing information right now to help you move toward something fun, interesting, exciting, and successful. It's your intuition. Saying "I don't know what do to next" shuts off the flow of intuitive information. Be willing to play with this idea. What if you did know what to do next? If you had a wise guide inside of you giving you clues, what would she or he be saying to you? If "I'm stuck" or something similar is in your mind and endlessly repeating itself, try replacing it with "I'm getting clearer" and "New ideas are coming every day, and I'm looking forward to following up on them."

Jenny was guilty of repeating the "I don't know" mantra. As soon as she began replacing that phrase in her mind, new possibilities presented themselves. She realized that the idea of offering pet-sitting services in her neighborhood appealed to her, and she took some steps toward that.

At the same time, she shared her interest in small-business marketing with her boss. Over the course of the next year, they implemented some of Jenny's ideas, which turned out to be highly successful. Her boss eventually created a new position for her. She was able to negotiate a flexible work schedule as well as an increase in pay. She now celebrates her new life with friends from her classes as well as a number of canine friends she takes for fitness walks around the neighborhood.

What do you do if you determine you're off track? As Yogi Berra said, "If you come to a fork in the road, take it!" What are you doing that's on the mark? If one way doesn't work for you, be ready to go another. Many times, the road to success is found by taking a detour. Sometimes we get overly focused on getting to our goals through a well-trodden or familiar path. A crisis is one of the ways that the Universe can show you a new direction. If you can say yes to the alternative route in

If you come to a fork in the road, take it!

front of you, you may find a wonderful new vista opening up that's full of opportunity.

It's worth noting that many of the people I interviewed for this book mentioned failures, detours, being stuck, and other life circumstances that ultimately served to get them on track. With enough distance, almost all of them were grateful for the setbacks because it allowed a whole new and more interesting life to emerge. They invariably mentioned that following their intuition was the guide that led them back to success.

Sometimes you have to look ahead to your future and not just back at your past. I was speaking with a client recently who was contemplating going back to school for a master's degree at fifty-three years old. She was the director of a high-profile nonprofit organization and had been in this position for fifteen years. She knew it was time to leave and yet was consumed with anxiety about whether the program she'd been accepted into was the right choice. Was her intuition telling her not to go?

I suggested she think of her life a year from now and asked, "How will you feel if you're still in your current job and you didn't go back to school?" Her instant reply? "Disappointed." Her response served to soften her anxiety. It made her realize that she was, in fact, heading in the right direction.

When you've put a lot of hard work into an endeavor and it's not going as you planned, it's not easy to step back and assess the situation. It may be time for a "performance review." Is there something that you feel you're failing at in your life? The following questions will help you put some perspective on your experience.

- What can I learn from this?
- What am I doing right?
- What outcome will make me feel that I'm successful?
- Where did this situation begin to go wrong?
- What do I wish I had done differently?
- What is my intuition telling me to do about this situation?
- What am I not listening to?
- What am I afraid will happen?
- What could I do to prevent this thing I fear?
- Are there warning signs I'm ignoring?

- What do I know I should do?
- Will a small step help? If so, what could I do?
- Is this the time I need to take a big, courageous step? If so, what do I need to do?

After answering the above questions, do you feel there's a different way to approach this situation? Depending on the issue, you have several options. You could:

- Quit. (Stop what you've been doing.)
- Persevere.
- Alter your course.
- Put the situation on hold for a period of time.
- Try something new.
- Ask for advice from someone who has been successful in a similar situation.
- Cut back on your involvement and see if some distance might help.
- Increase your involvement and try to resolve the situation.
- Discuss the situation with others who may be involved.

Which of these options feels best to you? You can choose more than one, and your intuition may present you with even more choices than are listed here.

Thomas J. Watson was the founder of IBM. He was one of the richest men of his time and considered one of the world's greatest salesmen when he died in 1956. I thought his words might provide some comfort for those experiencing a setback. "Would you like me to give you a formula for success? It's quite simple, really. Double your rate of failure. You are thinking of failure as the enemy of success. But it isn't at all. You can be discouraged by failure or you can learn from it. So go ahead and make mistakes. Make all you can. Because remember, that's where you will find success."

Did you know that whenever someone says,
"I think I'm on to something HUGE, I'm so excited,
I love my life, I have total clarity . . ." it's like hitting an
"On" button that throws countless supernatural,
invisible mechanisms into action that gradually
begin physically rearranging the props and events
of their life so that they'll soon yield something
HUGE, generate excitement, inspire love
and provide clarity?
—Mike Dooley

YOUR INTUITION JOURNAL

At the top of a blank page write, "I do know what to do. My next steps are . . ."

Sit in silence for a few moments and let your intuition deliver ideas, suggestions, and inspiration to you. When you feel ready, write the answers you've received.

As you write down what comes to you, pay attention to the ideas that have energy. Are there ones that you feel eager to do? Are there at least one or two that you feel interested in pursuing? Circle those. That's your intuition indicating your successful next steps.

CHAPTER 25

This Too Shall Pass

Nothing is predestined. The obstacles of your past
can become the gateways that lead to new beginnings.
—RALPH BLUM

One of the questions I ask in my "Life Transitions" survey is, "Is there a quote that you found helpful during your life crisis?" The winner by a wide margin was the phrase, "This too shall pass."

There are varying stories of the origins of this quote. The most popular is the one that comes from the biblical King Solomon. He was known for his wisdom, his wealth, and his writings. He became ruler in approximately 967 B.C., and his kingdom extended from the Euphrates River in the north to Egypt in the south. His crowning achievement was the building of the Holy Temple in Jerusalem. Almost all knowledge of him is derived from the biblical books of Kings I and Chronicles II.

It was said that King Solomon was going through a very difficult time and asked his jewelers to make him a ring he'd envisioned in a dream. On the ring he saw these words that gave him great comfort—gam ze ya-ah-vor. These are the Hebrew words for, you guessed it, "This too shall pass."

The sixteenth president of the United States, Abraham Lincoln, also used the phrase in a speech he gave in 1859. "It is said an Eastern monarch once charged his wise men to invent him a sentence to be ever in view and appropriate in all times and situations. They presented him the words, 'And this, too, shall pass away.' How much it expresses! How chastening in the hour of pride! How consoling in the depths of affliction."

Lincoln successfully led the country through its greatest internal crisis, the American Civil War, saving the Union and ending slavery. By all accounts he was a deeply sensitive man; we can only imagine the immense despair he must have felt sending tens of thousands of soldiers into battle. To keep himself calm and focused, he used this phrase throughout his term as president. He reminded himself that whatever was happening was temporary. It too would pass.

Helen Steiner Rice is often referred to as "poet laureate of inspirational verses." One of her most famous poems is "This Too Shall Pass." She was born in 1900, long after Lincoln made his speech. She had more than her share of ups and downs during her eighty-one years. She was born into a family of poor immigrants. Her father died during the flu epidemic of 1918, making her the breadwinner of the family at only eighteen years old.

She later married a wealthy banker and reportedly had a huge mansion, many cars, and a life of ease until the stock market crash of 1929 that began the Great Depression. Her husband lost his job during this time, resulting in massive debt. He ultimately committed suicide at the age of thirty-two, leaving Helen a young widow.

It was not easy for anyone to find work during the Depression, especially a young woman. However, Helen was eventually employed writing verses for a greeting card company. Her poems and other writings have comforted many people over the years. Here are some lines from her most famous one:

> *This Too Shall Pass*
> *. . . I can suffer whatever is happening*
> *For I know God will break all the chains*

Like Helen Steiner Rice, it's all too easy to assume that whatever you're going through is permanent. You fear your life will stay in this crazy, painful, and agonizing place forever. It's true that you can't bring a loved one back from death or change the fact that your spouse had an affair or that you were fired from your job. But what you can change is your response to it. And that can make all the difference.

Positive psychology is a new branch of psychology that studies the strengths and virtues that enable individuals and communities to thrive. Positive psychologists seek "to find and nurture genius and talent," and "to make normal life more fulfilling."

A large body of research from this positive psychology group reveals that people adapt to the circumstances in their lives, both good and bad.

For example, you win the lottery. You may be very happy for a short while, and then your happiness level will simply drop back to where you were before the big win. This has also been shown to be true when something bad or difficult happens. You experience a health challenge, the loss of a loved one, or some other big crisis. Grieving, sadness, and depression are normal responses—and yet, over time, people generally return to the level of content (or discontent) they experienced prior to the life event.

Happiness researcher and positive psychologist Ilona Boniwell completed a study of more than 1,000 people in the UK, asking, "What does happiness mean to you?" What was interesting is that 56 percent of the respondents equated happiness with contentment.

According to the dictionary, contentment is "accepting things as they are." Another interpretation is "mental or emotional satisfaction and foremost, a peace of mind." When survey participants were asked what contributed to their contentment, Dr. Boniwell received very practical and down-to-earth replies.

- "For me, happiness is about personal tranquility."
- "Happiness is going to sleep peacefully and waking up the next day."
- "It's about being at peace with the way things are going."
- "Happiness is when you are ok inside about where you are and who you are."
- "Happiness is taking the dog for a walk."

What struck me when reading about the study and the responses is that happiness and contentment are choices. As this survey's respondents suggested, it's the little things that can get you through the tough times. It could be cuddling with your cat or dog, taking a walk, looking at the stars, or getting a hug from a loved one. These things can all create contentment and can coexist even when you're in the midst of a crisis. When you're going through a difficult time, what makes you feel content?

Dr. Boniwell stated, "The trick is that what really matters is what's going on inside rather than outside. In other words, what we want depends on us, rather than the situation. By changing our perspective we can affect our level of contentment as much, if not more, as we could do by changing the situation. As a famous saying goes, 'change what you can, accept what you cannot and have the wisdom to know the difference.'"

So how can you expand the level of contentment and peace in your life even when you're going through an exceptionally tough time? According to the positive psychologists, practicing gratitude and consciously choosing constructive, uplifting thoughts will have a positive impact on your long-term health and happiness.

Make Note of the Good Things

While life crises often cause upset in many areas of our lives, all is not lost. Begin to pay attention to what is going well. One survey respondent told me about how overwhelmed she felt while her young daughter was in the hospital with a life-threatening illness. "I was so angry and bitter at God for letting her get sick that I was making myself ill from all those negative feelings. When I realized that, I began to consciously focus on what good things were happening each day."

She read a recent list to me that included, "My neighbor made dinner for us. Some of my daughter's test results indicated she was improving. My husband greeted me with a bouquet of flowers when I came home from the hospital and gave me a big hug." This woman noted that as her mood improved, she felt more able to be present with her daughter. She also felt that she was more open to intuitive guidance when she shifted her focus from lack to gratitude.

What's Good about Your Life?

It's all too easy to feel awful about how bad things are when you are going through a crisis. But even during a challenging time, there are good things happening to you and around you. For example, my husband is self-employed, and many of the companies he works with have experienced massive layoffs. He noted today that while some of his clients are calling less frequently, he's particularly grateful that they're all still using his services. Another positive psychologist, Dr. Robert Emmons, says this about the benefits of putting your focus on what you're happy about: "Gratitude elevates, it energizes, it inspires, it transforms. People are moved, opened, and humbled through experiences and expressions of gratitude." How about you? What's good about what is currently happening?

Take Time for Gratitude

Martin Seligman is considered the "father of positive psychology." He wrote about a wonderful technique in his book *Authentic Happiness*. He called it the Gratitude Visit. It goes like this: Pick a person in your life whom you'd like to thank, someone who has meant a lot to you. Write this person a letter. After you've written it, call the person and ask to visit. Read the letter aloud when you are face-to-face.

One woman I spoke with did a version of this at her mom's funeral. She went up to every friend and relative who had been close to her mother and shared a positive memory. "My mom had many wonderful friends during her lifetime and had equally wonderful stories about them. I felt like I was channeling my mom and her immense gratitude for life as I shared these moments with her loved ones who were still here. It helped me immeasurably in overcoming my grief and loss. My mom still feels very close to me because of this experience."

Practice the Glad Game

I once had a roommate who was a classic pessimist. We got into an argument one evening and, in a moment of pique I will never forget, she yelled at me—"You are pathologically positive!" I will cherish that to my dying days!

How did I come by this positivism? It was from the book *Pollyanna* that I read as a child. The title character is Pollyanna Whittier, a young orphan who lives with her wealthy but stern aunt Polly. Pollyanna's philosophy of life centers on what she calls The Glad Game, an optimistic attitude she learned from her father. The game consists of finding something to be glad about in every situation. It originated in an incident one Christmas when Pollyanna, who was hoping for a doll in the missionary barrel, found only a pair of crutches inside. Making the game up on the spot, Pollyanna's father taught her to look at the good side of things—in this case, to be glad about the crutches because "we don't need 'em!"

Accept That Life Brings Changes

Buddhism was founded in India 2,500 years ago and is the dominant religion of the Far East. The Buddha was driven to understand what caused suffering. "One thing I teach: suffering and the end of suffering. It is just ill and the ceasing of ill that I proclaim." One of his most important findings was that when people fail to accept the temporary nature of things, they suffer more than they need to.

This too shall pass. Everyone experiences change. It may take many forms—death, illness, loss, pain, uncertainty. It's a constant for all of us. You might consider using this phrase as your mantra, just as Abraham Lincoln and King Solomon did. You won't stay in this crisis forever. Your circumstances will change. Your feelings will change. Allow the transformation of your life, and trust that better times are coming your way.

It was humbling to read the responses to my survey. So many people wrote about their losses, fears, and crises. Yet person after person spoke about the triumph they felt at successfully navigating through these life challenges. They gained something that may have been missing in their lives. Coming from the hot, fiery embers of their worst nightmares, they spoke of finding their courage, their calling, true love, self-esteem, gratitude, compassion, forgiveness, and, yes, even their inner voice of wisdom.

One woman wrote, "I look back on the terrible time I've gone through and thank God that it is behind me. I'm amazed at my own strength and determination. I also come out of it whole with an appreciation for God's guidance. Without the still, quiet voice within, I'd still be left in the darkness."

You will find another job. You will discover friends, love, community, faith, and health again. You will survive until you die and pass into the next life, as we all must. The novelist Ernest Hemingway wrote, "The world breaks everyone, and afterward, many are strong at the broken places." May you be made strong even in your suffering.

When you get into a tight place and everything goes against you, till it seems as though you could not hold on a minute longer, never give up then, for that is just the place and time that the tide will turn.
—HARRIET BEECHER STOWE

YOUR INTUITION JOURNAL

Sit quietly with your journal nearby.

Choose a saying or statement that reminds you that the difficult time you're experiencing is transitory. Examples are, "This too shall pass" and "I know I'll get through this tough time and feel better again."

Close your eyes and say your chosen phrase quietly to yourself.

Notice how you feel as you say this calming statement. What do you notice in your body and emotions? Are there any images that come to your mind? Perhaps there's an inner whisper encouraging you and giving you a message.

When you feel ready, open your eyes and write about your experience and any inspiration you received.

CHAPTER 26

Making the Choice to Be Happy

If you think negative thoughts all the time, you're going to be crabby and miserable. If you want to be happy, recognize you have a choice. Choose positive thoughts!
—LORRAINE WATSON

My ninety-year-old mother-in-law inevitably comes to mind when I think of someone who's happy. She's the source of the above quote. She's a living example of choosing happiness despite challenging circumstances. In fact, her nickname is Rosie because of her wonderful disposition, which she maintains despite a host of problems, including macular degeneration, colon cancer, having to live on a fixed income, relying on others, and more.

Despite all this, she tells me, "Oh I am so glad to be alive! I just love sitting outside on the lawn and listening to the birds sing. I just sit there and think of all the things I'm grateful for. I pray every day for those people who don't have as much as I do. I have all my kids and grandkids living around me, and I feel so filled up with gratitude. I've lived a long time and God may take me anytime, but I'm just going to appreciate every moment I have left. I figure if I'm still above ground, then it's a good day. God must not be ready for me yet."

My mother-in-law is someone who clearly chooses happiness, and happiness has clearly chosen her. She focuses on all that she has to be grateful for and attracts more of its richness into her life. If my husband and I want to take her out to lunch, we have to schedule a date. We're not always first in line among the many people who like to hang out with her. Her happiness is contagious. It makes her very popular.

I told her recently that I admired her attitude of grace toward the process of aging. She said, "I accept it. I don't fight it. For example, my sight is almost gone. I've done everything I can to change it. I've prayed, gone to doctors, done the treatments, and it's still diminishing. Maybe my efforts slowed it down, maybe they didn't. I don't dwell on the fact that I don't have my sight. I simply take pleasure in the little that I can see. I know that whatever happens to me, I'll still be okay as long as I put my focus on being grateful and happy. That is what I have control over!"

I think Rosie would agree with former president Abraham Lincoln, who said, "Most people are about as happy as they make up their minds to be."

Who comes to your mind when you think of someone who's happy? It's probably not the wealthiest person you know, or the most famous. Those who sparkle with aliveness are ordinary people like you and me. Like my mother-in-law, they have not lost their wonder of the moment. They cherish the call from a friend. They delight at hearing a child laugh. They have times in each day when they stop and take a deep breath and simply appreciate the way things are. They listen to the breeze blowing through the trees, observe a bird flying, listen to their cat purr, and smell the flowers. They find a gift in each day they're alive.

Your Happiness Meter

Stop reading for just a moment and check in with yourself. How happy are you? Measure yourself on a scale of 1 to 10, where 1 is a feeling of being quite depressed, and 10 is elated and optimistic. What number would you choose?

Now I'd like you to ask yourself another question. "What could I do to feel better right now?" Don't think about it too much. Just take whatever quickly pops into your mind. It's likely to be something simple. You could stand up and stretch. Take a walk to the watercooler if you're at the office. You could opt for a quick nap if you're at home. You might pet your dog or cat or call a friend to say hi.

One of my students, Gene, shared a great story about how his father helped him become happier. Here's his story . . .

I had a period in my life where I was quite depressed. I had just graduated from college and was feeling pretty lost, lonely, and directionless. Like so many kids that age, I had been somewhat out of touch with my parents. I just touched base to do some laundry or grab a meal when I was home visiting them.

One particularly tough night, I realized that I really missed my dad a lot. When I was growing up I could ask him for advice and he'd always say something that made me feel better. It occurred to me that when I spoke with my dad, the situation I was discussing with him didn't change (at least not immediately), but I always ended our talks uplifted. He'd point out that I was telling myself a story about my life circumstances that made me feel discouraged, and he'd suggest a way to change it.

So I called him to complain about how difficult it was for me to find a job. I went on endlessly about the unemployment rate, the number of college friends I knew who couldn't find jobs, and how disheartened I felt. Finally he stopped me and said, "Gene, I read a statistic the other day. It said your graduating class has a 7 percent unemployment rate. What could you do to be among the 93 percent of your class who has a job?"

He didn't say it in an accusatory or blaming way. He stated the question in such a way that it really gave me pause. I wanted to honor the question with a thoughtful response. I told him I'd give some time thinking about this and would call him the next day.

It was interesting to watch my thoughts go from a whining, "Why can't I find a job? I'm doomed," to a much more empowered, "What can I do to find a job?" As soon as I shifted the question, I not only felt better, but answers began coming to me. I was able to report back to my dad the next day with several ideas. I took action on them and landed a great job within two months.

My dad died a few years ago and I miss him terribly. That conversation I had with him post-college was one of the most important we had. It helped me develop a technique that has greatly contributed to my happiness and contentedness in life.

When I begin to feel depressed, angry, upset, or any other unconstructive emotion, I ask myself a simple question. "What am I saying to myself right now that has me feeling unhappy?"

Usually the answer is pretty obvious—I'm dwelling on something negative. Once I know what it is I can do something to change the story I'm telling myself.

The next thing I do is to contemplate the question, "What could I do (or think) that would make me happier?"

If I'm going through a difficult period in my life, I actually write that last question out on a three-by-five card and stick it in my pocket. I find that my intuition will throw out answers throughout the day. It might come to me as an inner voice, a feeling, a knowing, or even as an image that leaps to mind. It makes me feel connected to my dad, and I like to think he's on the other side, still giving me advice and cheering me on. I always feel comforted by that thought.

Many of us go through life asking the wrong questions: "Why can't I make more money?" "Why am I unhappy?" Gene's dad taught him an important lesson about the most advantageous question to ask. When you put the focus on being happy, intuition flows in with inspirational direction and wise guidance.

Make Time for Fun

When you're going through a tough time like a painful divorce, an illness, or a financial crisis, it seems as if your world closes in on you. You can't see options or alternatives that could help you. Your mind is filled with thoughts of your situation and it's hard to imagine life being "normal" again. Do you know that it's possible, and even recommended, to have fun while you're going through a tough time? Those are not mutually exclusive ideas!

Years ago I was going through a particularly challenging time financially, physically, and emotionally. I was in a demanding master's in education program. I had cut back my full-time job to part-time, and between the tuition and my living expenses, I was barely making ends meet. In addition to that I was struggling with a medical condition that my doctors couldn't figure out.

At the time, I was dating a guy who was in a similar stressful situation and also experiencing financial problems. We came up with a "Most Fun/ Least Expensive Date" contest. The rules were simple. Find something really fun to do together that was ideally free, but not more than $5.

We both lived near Boston, so we had a lot of options. Here are some of the things we came up with and actually did:

- Attend summer concerts on the town green.
- Bird-watch in a wildlife sanctuary.
- Watch high school baseball games.
- Dance at an informal sock hop.
- Go to gallery openings.
- Have a potluck dinner with friends.
- Take a long walk with a friend's dog.
- Go to the beach and watch a sunset.
- Create gravestone rubbings at a historic cemetery.
- Volunteer at a soup kitchen.
- Visit a friend who has a new baby.
- Go to the library for film night.
- Attend a book signing and author's talk at a bookstore.
- Play board games.
- Make chocolate chip cookies.
- Ride bikes to the local ice cream parlor.
- Take a class on how to be a hospital clown.
- Visit kids in the hospital.
- Visit the museum during the "free day."
- Sing Christmas carols at a nursing home.
- Hear lectures from visiting professors and authors at local colleges.

I learned a valuable lesson during this time: Even though I was having a tough time, life could go on. My reality didn't need to be all about "my illness" or "my debt" or "my stressed-out school experience." As I'm writing about this time in my past, I realize the memory is more about the fun I had and less about all of the challenges I was experiencing. What could you do today to have fun?

The best remedy for those who are afraid, lonely or unhappy is to go outside, somewhere where they can be quiet, alone with the heavens, nature and God. Because only then does one feel that all is as it should be and that God wishes to see people happy, amidst the simple beauty of nature.

—ANNE FRANK

YOUR INTUITION JOURNAL

Consider creating a page in your journal for inexpensive, fun things to do. Add to the list whenever a new idea pops into your mind.

Start your day by asking, "What could I do today to be happy?"

Another great question is "What could I do today that's fun?"

(I love looking at those lists I've created from years past.)

Pay attention to any and all answers you receive. That's your inner wisdom at work. Take action on the ones that most excite you.

CHAPTER 27

Wise Guidance from Fellow Travelers

What once seemed like a curse has become a blessing.
All the agony that threatened to destroy my life now seems like the
fertile ground for greater trust, stronger hope and deeper love.
—HENRI J. M. NOUWEN

Ending a book is always tough for me. What's been left unsaid? What could I have said better? Are there any words of wisdom that could offer comfort to you, my reader, as you make your way through a period of crisis? I've decided to let others, like you, who have made it through a rough patch say it for me. Following are the top fifty wise messages I have heard most frequently from fellow travelers on the path—folks I interviewed for this book and clients who have shared their stories with me over the past twenty years. My deep, heartfelt thanks to all of you.

The Top 50 List of Wise Advice

1. When you've done all you can do and life still isn't going your way, it's time to surrender. God has a better plan. Make a space for His miracles.

2. Be extra-kind to yourself. If you're going through a crisis, it isn't the time to beat yourself up or get down on yourself for some perceived failing. Simply do the best you can every day. Things will get better.

3. When you begin to feel overwhelmed, stop. Wherever you are, take a few slow deep breaths. It will help you feel calmer and realign your spirit.

4. Have a positive, easy-to-remember affirmation that can get you through a tough day. My favorites are: "This too shall pass." "It

is what it is." "I let go and let God." "All I can do is put one foot ahead of the other and keep moving." "I am [or this situation is] in God's hands." And finally, "It will all work out."

5. When you don't know what to do, just take the next right step. It doesn't have to be a big leap.

6. Life is short. Don't waste it being bitter, dwelling in the past, or being angry with yourself or others.

7. All of us experience ups and downs in life. Don't compare your current life with others'. You have no idea what their journey has been.

8. Keep your focus on where you want to go, not on where you've been. All endings simply become new beginnings.

9. It's okay to cry. It's even better to cry with someone. Hugs and a reassuring presence make you feel less alone.

10. Medication and seeing a doctor or therapist for help is okay. Don't feel like you're weak if you need to take antidepressants, sleeping pills, or the like when you're going through a tough time. God's healing presence is in medicines, too.

11. Make a list of small pleasures. These could be getting your hair done, taking a walk with a friend, renting a funny movie. Do at least a few of them every week. It's important to take care of yourself even when you're in a crisis.

12. God's delays are not His denials. Be patient. The Universe is unfolding just as it should. You're being readied for something better.

13. Keep in touch with people who love you and make you feel better. Surround yourself with "yay-sayers," not naysayers. Life is too short to hang out with folks who make you feel bad.

14. If you're still here, God isn't finished with you yet. Hold to the thought that your crisis is just a temporary situation.

15. Don't be a victim. Be a victor. No one is in charge of your happiness except you. It's okay to have doubts and fears, just don't dwell on them.

16. At the end of your life, it's not the toys, the money, the positions you've held. The most important thing is that you loved and allowed yourself to be loved in return.

17. Spend time outside. You'll see that Mother Nature experiences a constant rebirth, and so can you.

18. Pursue your interests. That is your intuition speaking. Your interests are saying, "Choose me!" That's a clue to lead you to your next right step.

19. If something drains you or bores you, it's a sign that change is needed. It's also your intuition speaking. It's saying, "Move away from this," or "Don't go in this direction."

20. Find time to go within every day. Your faith may be in God, angels, Muhammad, spirit guides, Jesus, Divine Consciousness, or simply yourself. Seek the still quiet within to connect with Wisdom.

21. Ask for help. It can come in many forms—a close friend you can count on, a therapist, a member of the clergy, a support group, someone who has shared a loss similar to yours: Find a connection that's right for you. Community is an important component to help you heal and live your best life.

22. Take time to help others. Research shows that volunteering is helpful in healing depression. Often the one being helped the most is you!

23. Remember that you're an expert on yourself. Everyone will have advice for you—"Let it go." "It's time to get on with your life." "You should [fill in the blank]." But only you know what's right for you. Trust your own guidance.

24. If you lack confidence or suffer from poor self-esteem, do something each week that pushes you out of your comfort zone a little. It will help you develop your courage muscles and is the fastest way to build your belief in yourself and your abilities.

25. Go slow. Rest. Take it easy. Build downtime into each day. Your body and soul need time to heal. The precious buds of miracles often take root in the fertile soil of sleep, rest, and healthy food.

26. You may still be coping with an illness, a loss, or a disappointment; these things do not need to define your life. Joy, pleasure, and happiness can, and often do, coexist with pain.

27. Take the first step in faith. The power of the Universe will be there to support all future steps. You will be led in grace on the right path.

28. Check in daily with your intuition. Asking "what" questions is key. "What's my next step?" "What would make me feel better now?"

29. Look for the good. Know that life is always changing and that things can and will get better.

30. Keep your focus on the present moment. "In this moment, I am okay." When you're ready, expand that into hours, then days, then weeks.

31. Get out of your house. You can't figure everything out sitting in your home alone. You need to connect, be in community, step out of your comfort zone, and create new pathways for possibilities.

32. Take the next easy step. Do what's possible until you realize you're doing the impossible.

33. Be patient with the process of healing. Answers will come. They may arrive as a knowing or sometimes in the form of people and events.

34. If you don't know where you're headed, simply say, "Let me be open to new possibilities."

35. Practicing good self-care isn't selfish. It's the best thing you can do in your own time of need.

36. Write down in detail what you want your life to look, feel, and be like. Cut out images and words from magazines to create a visual collage of this new life. Spend time with these words and images every day until they become your life.

37. God is on your side. If you can remain peaceful within, the outside circumstances hold no power over you.

38. Let others have the opportunity to support and befriend you in your time of need. We're all in this together. Keep affirming "People want to help me." They do!

39. Sometimes the message to take it "one day at a time" is too much. Give yourself permission to cry, rant, and rave. If you can only take it a minute or an hour at a time, that's fine, too. Just keep loving yourself. You'll get through to the other side.

40. If you're faced with an emergency, sit down, center yourself, and pray. Ask for guidance. Receive it. Hear it and act on it.

41. Don't expect instant results. Making a change takes time. God is working on you from the inside out. Expect to be uncomfortable for a while. Make peace with not knowing.

42. If you have a tendency toward depression, get out of bed! The longer you lie there, the bleaker your outlook is going to be. Make yourself a cup of tea, feed the cat, call a friend, get out of the house and into the world.

43. Change your media viewing habits. There's nothing more depressing than watching violent television shows or listening to depressing economic woes when you're going through a tough

time. Rent some uplifting DVDs, program your iPod with uplifting music or podcasts, read some good books, ones that make you feel better. (Like Lynn's!)

44. Don't be a perfectionist, especially when you're going through tough times. Give yourself permission to have things be "good enough."

45. Take time for exercise. It boosts your endorphins and makes you feel better. Even if you can only walk a block, think of it as your intuition time.

46. Say things to yourself like, "I want to feel better" or "I could always just cheer up." Try it a few times. It sounds a little artificial, but it really works.

47. When you're in the grip of fear, try to let your awareness soften. Stop and listen. What do you hear? A bird singing? A car honking? A newspaper rustling? Taking your mind off your fear and putting it into the larger reality around you can often shift you away from your fear and into an oasis of peace.

48. Turn big decisions into small decisions. When you're in a crisis, everything tends to feel overwhelming. Put your focus on what's important. What small decision can you make right now?

49. Try turning your worries over to God. Accept that your worrying about every little thing isn't helping. Write your worries down and then put them in a box or write "surrendered to the Divine" across the note. It's a tangible way to "let go and let God."

50. Choose to feel calm. What if this crisis you are currently experiencing is really meant to bring you to a better place? Embrace the change and know that you'll come out the other side feeling more hopeful, strong, and optimistic. Real life begins at the end of your comfort zone.

So there you have it, my friends. Life is a journey. Sometimes the terrain is rocky and sharp. Sometimes it's even, open, spacious, and inviting. We all pray for the latter, but it's often the tough times with the roughest landscape that get us there.

You have within you an inner compass that will help you navigate through both the easy times and the tough times. You don't travel this journey alone. God is at the helm and sends direction, solace, helpers (seen and unseen), and support in even the darkest times. God's love surrounds you. Ask for help. Ask for wisdom. Ask for strength. Ask for your intuition to speak to you loud and clear. Ask to be in the flow of Divine wisdom.

My prayer for you is that you'll take time to turn within and listen. Trust your inner voice to guide you, and savor the many stops along your journey. It will all work out. I send you my blessings for courage, wisdom, and love.

The basic principle of spiritual life is that our problems become the very place to discover wisdom and love.
—JACK KORNFIELD

YOUR INTUITION JOURNAL

At the close of this book, what do you need to know? What questions are unanswered for you? Write them in your journal.

You have your own Divine wisdom that is always with you, guiding you, providing answers. You are never alone.

Take the time to move into silence. Slow down your pace. Let yourself feel a deep sense of peace. Life is unfolding perfectly just as it is. Entertain the idea that everything is going to work out okay.

About the Author

Lynn Robinson, MEd, is one of the nation's leading experts on the topic of intuition. She's a popular and widely recognized author and motivational speaker who works with businesses and individuals as an intuition advisor, offering insights into goals, decisions, and strategies. Clients usually call her when they're in the midst of change and transition.

Lynn has been recognized by *Boston Magazine,* where she was voted "Best Intuitive" by readers and editors. She's been sought out internationally by entrepreneurs and executives for her intuition advice and counsel. Her "Gut Truster" seminars prompted *USA Today* to write, "Robinson has been retained by companies large and small to help their employees learn to use their intuitive nature."

In Lynn's keynotes and seminars, she teaches that intuition is a ready source of direction available to all of us; an invisible intelligence that animates our world and helps guide our lives. When we follow its wisdom, we are led to success, happiness, and inner peace. She believes we all have the ability to access this power and develop it for practical use in everyday life, as well as for discovering and achieving long-term goals.

Lynn has authored five books on the topic of intuition, including *Divine Intuition: Your Guide to Creating a Life You Love* (DK Books, 2001). She's also the author of *Trust Your Gut: How the Power of Intuition Can Grow Your Business* (Kaplan, 2006), *Real Prosperity* (Andrews McMeel, 2004) and *Compass of the Soul: 52 Ways Intuition Can Guide You to the Life of Your Dreams* (Andrews McMeel, 2003.) Her books have been translated into more than a dozen languages.

She has been featured in the *Boston Globe, USA Today,* and the *Chicago Tribune,* and has been a guest on many national radio and television programs including ABC, Fox News and the Wisdom Television Network. She's also been quoted in such publications as the *New York Times, Investor's Business Daily, Woman's Day, Redbook, Glamour, Self, Good Housekeeping, Woman's World, More,* and *First for Women.*

Lynn is an active member of the National Speakers Association and a sought-after motivational speaker who helps people make changes and achieve their goals—both personally and professionally—by following their intuition. With more than twenty years of speaking experience, she consistently receives high marks for the depth of her content; the good-natured, down-to-earth style in which she delivers it; and her winning sense of humor.

Lynn lives in suburban Boston with her husband, Gary, and their cat Sophie. As much as they love New England, they enjoy spending winters in Sarasota, Florida.